Heart of a Lamb
Courage of a Lion

Boab Curran

Copyright © 2013 by Boab Curran.

Library of Congress Control Number: 2013900648
ISBN: Hardcover   978-1-4797-7538-5
              Softcover   978-1-4797-7537-8
              Ebook   978-1-4797-7539-2

All rights reserved. No part of this book may be reproduced or transmitted in any form or by any means, electronic or mechanical, including photocopying, recording, or by any information storage and retrieval system, without permission in writing from the copyright owner.

This book was printed in the United States of America.

To order additional copies of this book, contact:
Xlibris Corporation
0-800-644-6988
www.xlibrispublishing.co.uk
orders@xlibrispublishing.co.uk

What is hurt, what is pain, let me tell you and hope it does not rain.
Hurt began every Friday, Pay Day, Father drinks it on the way home,
We might as well be targets against Lions in Rome.

Mother afraid but asks what is left ?
As usual the answer left us bereft, it's on the favourite at 4.29
If it wins we can buy some Wine. What about food for the week said she?
A Slap and Scream are what we heard first, blood and tears Mum needed a nurse.
Then the hard work began, choosing, who is leaving or staying with Dad.
Two of us left and two of us stayed. Why did it always had to be that way?
It made us mad, and now we know, it will always be that way.
No reckless abandon, fun or games, it hurts, it hurts, but won't give the game away.

He died on the day man went to the moon,
For us it was not a minute to soon.
Mum was a victim, and so you see her choice in men, seemed to be always that way.
It continued with others, until the day I went away.
To the Army at 15 a CHANCE I pray!

Little I was, and a champion too, that meant nothing to the paedophile zoo,
They buggered me and made me aware, I didn't have a man who really did care.
The police don't believe me, so what is the point? I will get them my way don't worry
I became a top boxer, because I felt the need to prove myself.

I drove myself almost obsessed, with the vision in my head I was gonna make rest.
A British champion I became, in 73, believe me, this was not for Me.
An Army Commando too, just to prove I was not him,
I am not him, but the person within.
My Army career died because I couldn't get the rage within, In a corner to settle whilst I tested my mettle,
Regrets I have many and not just a few.
However I am me, not you, and I am not going to that Zoo!!!!

© Bob Curran 05Jun 2012

CONTENTS

Chapter 1:   What a Start! 9
Chapter 2:   The Counting House..17
Chapter 3:   Becoming a Victim 25
Chapter 4:   The Bullying..31
Chapter 5:   St John's R. C. Secondary, The Traumatic Years 1966-70......35
Chapter 6:   My Dad, the Family, Life, and Demise 41
Chapter 7:   Chepstow—the Happy Years—Section 1 45
Chapter 8:   Chepstow the Happy Years—Section 2.............................50
Chapter 9:   Chepstow, the Happy Years—Section 3 56
Chapter 10: Chepstow, the Happy Years—Section 4 61
Chapter 11: Chepstow, the Happy Years—Section 5 66
Chapter 12: Cove, the Learning Curve 71
Chapter 13: First Training Regiment and Corporals' Mess....................76
Chapter 14: The Chattenden Years..81
Chapter 15: 1974 Pre-Fifty-Nine Commando Year 89
Chapter 16: The Fifty-Nine Years Commando Course and All............92
Chapter 17: Fifty-Nine Years, My First Beat-up...................................97
Chapter 18: The Citadel Instructor, Army Show, and Condor Troop ...101
Chapter 19: Fifty-Nine Cdo RE, the Defining Year 105
Chapter 20: Cyprus and It's All Over 109
Chapter 21: Going Home To What? 113
Chapter 22: The Saving Grace 118
Chapter 23: Letting Go!...122

CHAPTER 1

What a Start!

Do you know what? Evil bastards know they are evil bastards, but I had no clue, except I knew my dad was one!

Having been battered from my first memory does not give me the right to continue the practice. I have been informed that evil is too shallow a word to express my type of behaviour. My name is Bob Curran. I thought I was just an average person in a very under-average dump, just doing what most of the working class do . . . *get by*!

This book however will attempt to put my life back into a 'worth living' slot, because if it does not, I see absolutely no use in preparing a bijou old folks' room for me, for as they sing in *M.A.S.H,* 'suicide is painless'. I am just not preparing my time on earth for that great highlight: sitting medicated and drooling in front of a large flat screen TV with no choice of what I want.

First Memories

I was playing in our nice garden in Gourdie Terrace, aged three, and turned to see a gun flying towards my head-butt first, it made contact with my head (which was not yet the piece of concrete it now is), creating a gash which introduced me to Hospital Emergency and needle and thread for the first time. Unknowingly, I was going to get to know these establishments intimately. My mum had thrown the toy gun because I wouldn't come in. God, she had enough on her plate with my philandering father, who was either in the nerchant navy (safety), in a jute mill (safer), or in the pub (*danger*): System goes into overload.

My father, unknown to himself, had a massive brain tumour, which caused my glee the day man landed on the moon: 20 July 1969. When Dad was sober, he was great. He would take me fishing or hunting for rabbits, taught me to ride a bike, and played with us for hours. If he was going drinking in the country, he would arrange for us to go and play in the park, usually in Errol, Perthshire, amusing ourselves outside country pubs while he and his 'friend' imbibed to saturation point. I got to know every part of his only car: a green Hillman, registration plate KSA 117. Isn't it funny how you always remember funny stupid details like that? Whilst awaiting the demon, I would drive this wee car's imaginary flight plan to anywhere, fiddling with every button and knob, in anticipation with fingers crossed and every sense sharpened so that I knew which way to dodge should I not return everything to the exact state it was in. He was a keen bodybuilder and had all the equipment to compete with Charles Atlas in his bedroom. It must have cost a small fortune and, of course, it was sacrosanct, except when he was showing off. He was built like a brick shithouse, had black curly hair, and was good looking too—and he knew it. His ego was such that everyone else in the family, right down to my own kids, have self-esteem problems. My pals in those innocent days were Andy Lynch, Billy Smith, and Alma Burns, who lived opposite me. Hers was one of the homes of refuge on rough weekends. I am still in contact with Billy, who I am sure knows more about Rab than I do. His dad (Alfie) was Rab's best pal, who, being older, worked at keeping my dad safe from himself, defusing situations, and curbing the excesses as best he could.

There were days when we were absolutely brassic. Sorry, change that; there were months when money was very short. Dad was in the merchant navy; however, he only ever sent £10 a week, not a lot for Mum and three kids at that time, especially when rent and utilities took a major proportion of that. I used to walk for miles down the railway track, picking up bits of coal, bringing it home, and creating some heat.

The abuse I took from my peers, for this could never ever be underestimated, but they were not like us. They had the standard parents, who worked, spent time as a family unit, whereas my mum had to work so hard as a single parent, she worked part time sometimes stretching hours for more money and yet had to come home and do everything. Such was the strain. She was pregnant with Valerie and was home from work and busy doing the washing in the kitchen sink, no machine. I spotted a milk bottle which I assumed stupidly was water. Yes, huge swallow of caustic bleach. Mum made me be sick by drinking a wee drop of salt water, then kept me drinking water for what seemed an eternity; eventually and thankfully, she had did exactly the right thing. Can't remember if I managed to eat any food that night!

When she left for work in the morning about 7 a.m. after making me toast for when I got up, as the youngest two were at the McFee's, I would move immediately to the Ogierman family. I was always a self-survivalist, even on some days waking them up to get my porridge breakfast. Alex was always looking after me during the primary years. Mrs Ogierman used to say, 'Bobby, we like you coming, but 'please let us get up first!'

There was however a type of peace. Mum used to go to Bingo to try and win something, but wins were rare, and subsequently, money was even less. Tea would be five to seven chips counted and two slices of spam. Our sandwich was a roll of a chip round the spam and imagined *bread*! We used to sit and watch our wee monochrome TV as a fatherless family: laugh, joke, feel free to be ourselves. One night, we were watching a film *The Spiral Staircase*, directed by Robert Siodmak, when just at the critical moment, my father, who was out, waited until a certain second and banged on the back window. I crawled inside myself to survey the detritus that was coming; we were all screaming with fear and alarm. He was meantime rolling on the floor laughing his head off.

We were incredibly fortunate in our neighbours at that time. As I lie here, thinking about my early years, I have come to realise that of all the things we need in our lives, I would plump for neighbours who care each and every time. They weren't blind to our situation; they put up with a lot, me vandalising cars, letting tyres down, painting red cars black. We even had a mobile shop that came around the estate, and Ali, not knowing any better, would allow me to sit in his driver's seat, whilst others were being served, that is, until I somehow let the handbrake off and the said van began rolling down the hill.

They never ever rushed to tell tales, knowing the demon would probably end up extinguishing my backside from this planet. As I said, to me, he was a demon most of the time. Being the eldest, it was simple to pick on me!

At four, I was obsessed with the rear of the fish-and-chip shop in Brownhill Place. Dick, the manager, with a face built from stone, used to chase me. Then one day, he asked me to come in but watch my f—ing feet, as the place swims with water during prep time. He showed me a machine that peeled the potatoes (Note: no health and safety tosh in them days!). Then he said that if I came in and eyed the potatoes that came out of it, he would 'see me all right'. Dick was as good as his word: a bag of chips, or if I was lucky, a mock chop supper. This stopped me fighting for food at home, though I never let on why this was the case.

At nearly five, my small body was dragged to St Clement's Primary School in Charleston and I met 'Satan's Sister' for the first time, Sister Mary Angela (That name will go to the grave with me). I was very poor, to the point that I came across bullying and Prejudice for probably the first time. I ran away from home as regular as clockwork with my first toothbrush, which I received at school in Primary 1, when everyone had the real pleasure to meet one of the most sadistic dentists ever, who in a previous life could well have been pulling teeth in prisoner of war camps: no anaesthesia, nothing, unless you were getting back teeth out. You were then sent to Ancrum Road and given gas.

I would turn up at 21 Dryburgh Crescent or 77 Garry Place (grandparents) with a frequency to match the meal clock, always to be fed and watered, 1/-5p (5 pence) placed in my pocket and put on the bus home.

Mum meanwhile got a full time job to try and improve our income, as the tarts in some tropical country obviously had Dad's. Nanny McFee (really her name!) was employed to look after Kate and Tam, but she wouldn't as much as give me a drink of water after school. It was cold and dark till Mum got home, but never once was I permitted into the Mcfee household. I had to kick stones and cans about till Mum finished, only to get a clip and a 'Look at the state of your school shoes!' which my grandmother had bought, along with my first uniform, from a local Provident man.

Anyone born a Catholic will either understand or condemn my next fact: From Day 1, we were encouraged to give money to 'the black babies'. It was done in such a way that guilt always took over. We were given a card with thirty spaces in it, each space worth a penny. When the card was filled, you got a smile from a member of the S.S. and got another card to fill. It took me an awful long time to fill a card, as I never had cash, and it was casually mentioned that wee Bobby Curran was not trying to assist the poor black babies, and the bullying, psychological and physical, ensued.

Anyway, back to black baby tin. Sister Mary Angela used to gather the cash, throw it into a tin, and meticulously count it out at dinnertime. It struck me that if I went into class at playtime and pinched a couple of pennies, I could return it the next morning as a donation. It worked, and I wasn't getting bullied, my cards were filling like everyone else's, and I even got my name in the diocese magazine for filling three cards.

Then, like every entrepreneur, I got greedy. I would take a shilling from the box and hand back 6d and get some sweets with the remainder.

One day, I was leaving school, going to sit on the bin at home, when I saw my old man back from sea. He grabbed hold of me and beat me. Then when he got me home, he took off the dreaded belt and stripped my body of skin, even my knuckles and knees were grazed. Only then did he tell me it was for stealing from the black babies' tin.

I said, 'Well, if I got money, it wouldn't have to happen', but that just got another slap. I went back to school in bits the following day, and Sister Mary Angela was giggling with joy when she grabbed my very sore body and slammed it repeatedly against the blackboard, yelling, 'Thief—truant—useless boy!' I repeat, the object of this when I was five, with no money at all, was being battered for trying to be the same as others and support black babies probably better off than me!

We were also brainwashed, as that is the correct term, that the Catholic Church was the largest in the world. There would be a pie chart on the wall, and nearly five-eighths of it was Catholic. So why did we usually lose the St Patrick's Day annual rumble with Charleston Protestant School? Anyway, that is neither here nor there. We had to start going to church on Sundays, firstly to Wellburn Home, as St Clement's was not built, then to St Clement's. There was no roll call, as the nuns knew well who had been to church. They would ask the inevitable question, 'Who was saying Mass?' There were only two priests, so you had 50 per cent chance, and they would ask 'What colour was his vestments?' There were six colours, I believe, so the hands that were up, who were there, mostly me and a few others, would guess the colour. If you got it right, you were fine, if wrong, it was two strokes of the belt. Poor Steve Conway, he was colour blind and went to church religiously, even sitting beside the nuns, as if to say, 'I'm here.' Every Monday morning, he would go to those who were always there and ask what colour the robes were. So-called Christian children thought it was funny to tell Steve the wrong colour. As a result, he got belted as much as I did, and I didn't go. It was Primary 3 before you got colour-blind tests; only then did they realise. As Steve is my pal, I can assure you he was never given an apology for being wrongly strapped!

Sister Mary Angela could be so kind. Once I found a thick tube in her drawer and asked her what it was. She told me to keep out of her drawer and belted me with her dress tunic wrap belt, which didn't really hurt. The very next day, she asked me to go in and get a new jotter (*the drawer!*). Nah, no way was I going in there.

'Go to the drawer and get a new jotter.'—I refused, telling her I wasn't permitted. She then gave me two strokes from the real belt in the drawer. Not so funny, I can assure you, all for the sake of preserving her long thick tube. Anyway, I determined never to ask her for anything again. I was bruised all over, laughed at, and derided at every occasion. It wasn't going to happen again if I could help it.

When my parents were going out, they would always have a relative babysit us. I would normally be tied to the stairs by my uncle Denis, now deceased, as I was a real pest, wondering why he had a woman downstairs, yet I was in bed. One weekend, they could not get a babysitter. I was eight, Tommy six, Kathleen would be three or four, and my dad took us all to the Astoria Cinema, paid everyone in, and gave me money for sweets, etc., telling me to get out of the pictures at the very end and catch the last bus home. However, Kathleen, three, had never been in such a place before and was really scared, especially when the cowboys caught the Indians or whatever and you had everyone stamping their feet. She had defecated and was stinking. I had no choice but to take everyone out of the cinema and get the Number 28 back to Charleston. Not being aware of what to do for two hours, I first of all cleaned Kath's bum with her pants and threw them in the bin. I immediately thought of stone-faced Dick in the Brownhill Road chip shop; I knocked on the back door, so as not to bring attention to everyone. Eva, a friend of my mum's, answered. We must have looked like poor wee souls, as she ushered us into the back office. I looked at the clock; it was only 8 p.m.! I was going to get it big time. Anyway, Dick came into the back shop. As you know, he had known me all my life. He asked me to explain, which I did, as I am telling you. He then tried to call a couple of hostelries in Lochee, at the same time telling Eva to give us all something to eat and a drink. He was desperate not to call the police, but they couldn't be traced. Dick had no option; he after all had his business to run. Well, the upshot was that the police didn't come to see us but toured the Lochee hostelries and got my parents. Dad was livid; the veins were sticking out of his neck.

'Can't you do a simple thing when asked?' he asked.

The police told him that it was enough, as it wasn't me at fault and to be grateful for a son who thinks! Needless to say, I walked the 250 yards from Dick's chip shop with the other two kids really scared, and Mum said to Dad, 'Rab, you can't blame Bobby!'

His response was, 'Shut the fuck up, or you are next!' So for another 150 yards, I knew I was getting it. I had actually wet myself from fear, so first, I got a hiding, and secondly, he made a nappy to disgrace me further, which I was forced to wear to bed. I woke up in the morning; the nappy was dry, but all up my back it was wet. Tommy, through fear, wet the bed. You will never guess whose fault that was. Yes, you have it in one: *mine!*

When Dad was home, he used to make some of the meals to allow Mum some rest. I remember saying as we sat at tea, 'Dad, he's got more chips than me!'

I could see a glint of anger in his eyes, and he said, '*Right!* I will make you more chips. If you don't eat them, all you are for it!'

He got out the potatoes, peeled and chipped them, and he filled the old style chip pan with my victims. It was really full, as I could see the lard spitting and glistening and the sun coming into the kitchen window making the hot lard look almost magical! Anyway, after ten minutes, Dad called me back through and said, 'Right, get on with it!'

Simple. I knew how to eat loads; you took it like a marathon. I kept eating till the last morsel was off my plate. I then cheekily turned to Dad and said, 'What's for pudding?'

He burst out laughing and gave me probably the biggest cuddle I can ever remember.

I wrote to Archbishop O'Brien with Chapter 1 included and got this reply:

Cardinal O'Brien to Bob

Dear Bob,

I thank you for your email to me of 27 July 2012.

I assure you that I read the first chapter of your book very intently. It is indeed a very sad story and one which I found hard to believe. However, be assured I did believe every word of it.

Obviously there is nothing I can do now to help, but perhaps your book will indeed help others. Hopefully, in this present day and age, young people will not have to suffer in the way in which you did. You are indeed in my thoughts and I hope that life is treating you better at this present time.

> With good wishes to you,
> Yours sincerely in Christ,
> + Keith Patrick Cardinal O'Brien
> Archbishop of St Andrews and Edinburgh

CHAPTER 2

The Counting House

Seven years old, I was deemed old enough to walk into Lochee, to get my gran's messages. The list consisted of ten or fifteen items, and I had to go to Lipton's. This was a very busy, old fashioned store, which even had delivery boys on bikes. It was not heavily staffed, therefore always had one checkout off and one empty aisle.

So I instantly worked out a method of making money. I put my grandmother's message bag straight into the trolley and put all her shopping in the bag, always marking down the cost of the item. At the conclusion of my 'shopping', I would push the trolley through the empty aisle and walk out the shop. Two hundred yards towards my grandmother's house, there was a roundabout with a toilet block and a bench in the centre between the Ladies and Gents. Unbeknown to me, there were loads of weirdos hanging round there. Luckily, I never used the toilets.

However, that was my 'Counting House', where I would count the cost of the shopping and then calculate to the penny the exact 'take for the week'. (Yes, I was that bright!) I would then go to a more local shop with Gran's ten-shilling note and get her cigarettes (no age limit in 1962). I would then have loose change to reward myself and give Gran her correct change!

Then Gran would try and get me to accept more money. I would refuse all the time, saying, 'You do enough for me, Gran!'

I had just begun to get an interest in the large blue hut in Thompson Park at the end of Dryburgh Crescent. Then one day, the realisation of what it was started to change my life. The front door was never opened; however, on one sunny evening, it was. There was a boxing ring, and in it, two international class boxers were in the ring (Frank Gilfeather and Stuart Ogilvie ABA Champion 1969-71). I was hooked instantly and knew I wanted, more than anything, to attempt this sport. It just mesmerised me, watching those two young men match each other's skills. Since I was being bullied at Primary School, I immediately asked for permission to join. I was told the cost and cried. Where would I get 6d (2.5P) a night to learn this? My granny noticed me being upset and asked the reason.

She said, 'Don't worry. I got a new job last month. I am now washing Lochee United's football strips. I will pay it for you!'. *Result*. I had noticed the new washing machine (twin tub), but on weeks of really muddy weather, I really earned that money. Plastic sandals, our footwear for all weathers, were not good at preventing dirt getting to your feet. Hey, did I care? I was getting taught to box. She got the machine, plus ten pounds a week to wash, dry, and iron them. I dare anyone to tell me there was a better turned-out team in Dundee in 1962. Mary (my gran) was afraid to block her machine, so she put the strips in the deep sink beside the mangle (an old-fashioned spin dryer) in hot water and washing powder, where I had to get in and stamp on the strips; it was good fun and had a profound effect on my feet; they were clean!

I also remember the craziest thing. Dad was working in Dundee when we were getting ready for moving home, as our lovely house was too small. We would never use the coalman service, as it was too expensive. The post office 400 yards away sold twenty-eight-pound bags of pre-packed coal. Dad was training and posing upstairs. Mum asked him to go. She was heavily pregnant, and his response was to send Bobby. There I was, seven years old, going to carry twenty-eight pounds of coal home. The lady in the post office was shocked, but I had the money, and she had a business. I, like a man, toiled and picked up the bag and struggled out of the shop. I knew the possibility of me carrying it was nil. I crossed the road and then hit on a great idea. I would become a penguin and shuffle home. I put the bag of coal on my sandals and actually shuffled the whole way home. It must have looked funny, like a scene from a Charlie Chaplin movie.

Now, I know I was never an angel; I received and expected my fair share of telling-offs, this perhaps the worst one ever. I was in the drying green, wrestling with Andy Lynch. My mum asked me to go to the shops and get her 5 Bristol Cigarettes with her final 10d or 4p in today's currency. That night was 'pay night', or at least what was left.

I was boiling; it was always me. Anyway, as I walked around to the shops, a bus just stopped at the bus stop to pick up waiting passengers, and without a second thought, I jumped on and bought a 1d ticket to Dundee. Once on the bus, I had already terrified myself about the inevitable outcome. I got off the bus in the town and decided to go to the pictures; I went into the Forest Park Cinema, paying the 2.5d and telling the manager that my mum had sent me there till she went a message!

Anyway, I sat trembling and crying, knowing I was in the second deepest mire since the black babies debacle eighteen months before! Next thing I knew, I had wet myself, and there was a policeman speaking to me and asking me where I lived. Without even thinking, I said 77 Garry Place, Downfield. My beloved Granny Curran, she would see me OK, as No. 1 grandson. No, she did not; she slapped my face (the first and only time) and gave the policeman my address. She then said, 'Bobby, I am sorry, son, but you have everyone worried, and you're getting it . . . ' I did.

Only a fortnight later, we moved home to a tenement in Craigmount Road, all for an extra room for the girls. I was still doing the Lipton's Shopping and had just been caught by the police about the same time that I had been given the hiding for the 'Bristol' story. I must have got away with it for six weeks. Then the time came to be caught. I had been watched from the minute I walked into the shop. Yet the funny thing is I decided

I had to stop; however, if I stole the bacon and eggs only, just to give me a wee bit of cash (a bit like the junkie cutting down), I was paying that day. I got in the queue with all the Lochee (wives) ladies and waited my turn proudly in the queue. When I got to the checkout, the lady asked for my bag to pack for me.

Of course, I said, 'I am perfectly able to pack a wee message bag.'

The lady said, 'I Know.' Att that, a manager appeared from nowhere, took my bag, and grabbed me by the arm, telling the operator to charge the items and fill the bag, so the lady gets her food! I was dragged through to an office where they had a window through which you could look into the store, however could not be seen from the store side. I was required to sit and await the police. The operator brought the filled bag of messages up and took the money from me, returning enough change for Gran's cigarettes. It did not bother me too much at the time; however, there was the disgrace of being marched through Lochee with a big policeman either side of me and one very kindly carrying the evidence. On arrival at Lochee Police Station, I received the customary kick up the backside. I was used to them though and I kind of deserved it, for there was a police taxi to Dryburgh Crescent.

Please do not think I had no fun moving to Craigmount Road. It worked out well; it was a tenement shared with five other families fairly harmoniously. Across Buttars Road was a large cornfield where we rolled flat an area with our bodies to become a field for football, cricket, and anything else, like rounders. Tom McMillan and Alec McBreartie had the kind of leadership aura that I lacked and ensured no one was picked last every time for any team. We always tried to have the Martin brothers in the same team, as Peter, Billy, and David were so competitive they put me to shame. I have never seen anyone cry when a goal was called offside or no foul given when they were brought down; there would be instantaneous screaming matches. The funniest ever was playing cricket; we manipulated the game so that Davie would come into bat at dusk. We would allow him to get a few runs on the board; then suddenly a wide ball would be bowled. The wicketkeeper, usually me, would then pull the catgut tied to the bails, and Dave would be given out. The screams would start immediately, 'It's impossible! That ball was three feet wide!' Tears would roll down his face and anger came to the top. 'You bunch of cheating b*stards!' The tirade could last up to ten minutes, by which time we had to go home, as the street lights had come on . . . happy days.

South of the 'Swampy' there was an amazing old block of twenty houses that had two spiral staircases and four outside toilets for about 100 people.

There was an old lady living in the top west flat who had refused to move from her home, perhaps as all her life memories were there. Anyway, every other flat was fair game to us, knocking holes in the floors and walls to make our own indoor assault course. She used to come out occasionally and rant at us, so we called her Witchy Poo (terrible of us). No excuses, as children, you just want to do things differently. We would wait till we saw her get on the Number 29 bus and just invade the other nineteen flats. It was great fun making out we were firemen and other such people. Then we noticed the roof was still laden with 'tinkers gold' *lead*, simple to tear, has a very low melting point, and is a few quids' worth after Frank Kelbie (the scrap merchant) took his cut. We had our own processors. Team 1 would strip the lead, being careful not to touch 'Witchy's' house. Across the road on the railway line, there was a tiny little hut where many things went on. At that time, though, that was our metal ingot line. I would build a fire by pinching a couple of firelighters from Mum and soon was melting the lead using a bean tin cut in half to melt the lead, then pour it into syrup lids so that each ingot was the same. Whilst we did this, we had Team 3, who would build a haystack and jump from the hut roof into the haystack, watching for the policemen, who would kick our backsides.

Two hundred yards east of our pitch, we had two old-fashioned water holding tanks, with a central wall between them. They were covered in algae from neglect. We saw this as an excellent assault course, tying together barrels and planks. There was a tree right in the west corner of our 'Swampy'. Obviously, this was also good for a laugh. Many shoes were lost and we got many hidings for being soaking wet. I would not have changed it though. We, in effect, had our own community centre using old bits and pieces. Honestly, if I was offered my childhood again minus the paedophilia or live now with iPods, iPads, and computers, the decision would be simple. Take me back every time!

My dad was giving me grief after my summons came in, saying I was going to a bad boys' home called a borstal and generally doing the correct thing, scaring me witless. Then this incident occurred: Dad was on back shift and I had just had a bath, as I was going to see the chief of police the following day for, as my dad said, 'the borstal'.

I was scared. I mean really scared and had my dressing gown out of Mary McConnachie's Jumble Shop tied tightly around my waist as a comforter. Dad had asked my mum to let me stay up and watch *Z Cars* just to wind me further. I really was so scared that I could not sit and was standing in front of the roaring fire. (Dad was home working, rather than in the Navy, which meant we had coal.) We had no fireguard and my dressing gown went up in flames. I started to scream, and Mum came through. Seeing what had happened, she panicked a bit and tried to unknot the robe. She then ran to the kitchen and came back throwing pots of water at me. My screaming brought two of the neighbours down. Luckily, they knew how to douse the fire by rolling me on the ground. First though, they had to calm me and stop me running like a fiery banshee. Eventually, they doused the flames. The doctor came and said I had been very fortunate. I had a brown blistered bum, but it was superficial and would heal with a few days on my belly!

Next morning, with my blistered bum and my parents, we attended Bell Street and met the chief constable. He put the wind up me, showed me the cells, and said, 'It is perhaps the next step, unless you write and apologise and do not do the shopping for a few months'. I wrote my letter of apology and promised I would not do it again. Up till now, I have not gone back on this promise!

How, though, would I make the few extra pennies I would thieve normally? 'The Tipperary', the vast area which was rundown and used to house the migrant Irish jute mill workers, was by then really run-down, and as I wandered down the railway line, looking for orchards as well as coal, I came across a dingy little workshop which was producing bundles of kindling sticks. It looked simple; you put in enough sticks to pack the metal mould, pulled a large metal handle to tighten them together, then tied the bunch with string! So I asked the gaffer, a right 'fly by night', for a job. He laughed, got a box for me to stand on, and said it was piecework, as if I was meant to know what that was. The rate was 1/—a hundred bunches, and you had to do fifty an hour! Even on the box, it was a case of me to wee. I managed thirty in the first hour and twenty-five in the second hour. So had assumed I would receive 6d (2.5p). However, he said, 'Time up. Go home.'

I asked where my 6d was.

He said, 'Son, you don't understand. You haven't done 100, so you get nothing.'

At this, I went and got the jute knife and began unstringing my bundles. Next thing I knew, I was outside in the fresh air with only splinters in my fingers for my two hours' effort, never mind another learning experience, yet still only seven!

Boxing Training: In August 1962, I began my boxing career. I loved hitting the bags and watching myself throw punches in the mirror. I spent many months begging Jim Monroe to get me a fight, and eventually, in January 1963, I was brought to Brechin in a car to box for the first time.

I was so excited. In those days, scales for kids were not necessary, and so I stood beside my first opponent, Alan Crighton, and was thus matched. I was so proud getting into the ring in the light blue vest of Camperdown and baggy wee shorts and my brown plastic sandals. After three one-minute rounds, I was defeated and in tears. I was sure I had won, but my wee silver steel medal cheered me a little way. My first three fights were against the same opponent and I lost all three. It came out in later years that I only lost as his club chairman was President of the Midlands Boxing District! After boxing training, me and my pal, Peter Wilson, would race each other home playing scissors, stone, paper to decide who went down Pitalpin Lane, which was supposed to be haunted.

I do not know if it was but soon learnt the person who ran that way always won the race! About a month later, there were five of us, all the same age and roughly the same weight, at the club, which made good sparring.

Jim Monroe picked two to box on a show, and I was not selected; now that really hurt me, so I decided to move to Lochee Boys Club, my old next-door neighbour's club. It was situated in a dilapidated old YMCA, where the shower was a bucket of cold water thrown over you; thank goodness my testes were tiny then. I just loved this old club, as there were all sorts of sports going on: football, weightlifting, gymnastics, of course boxing, and a swimming night across the road in Lochee Public Baths. I could never get enough fighting then, and at night, me and another friend, Allan Smith, who lived underneath me, we would spar in the common close, with the walls as the ropes. Now Allan was a good four inches taller and twenty pounds heavier, so when he whacked me on the ropes, my head would thump into the brick wall, hardly an easy taster. However, we ironed out our boxing problems, and indeed personal ones, most winter nights on 25 Craigmount Road. I turned into a southpaw, right hand-leading counter puncher, because Allan hit so bloody hard. We both learnt many things in that close, which would come to fruition on 7 April 1969, when we both won Scottish Junior Titles.

Perhaps a week or two after Alan and I had won our titles, a brash, mouthy teenager turned up at our club (Many years later, he was to become an MP. I believe he left the Labour Party and just used his catchphrases about indefatigability and licking milk from a bowl on Big Brother. He then toured the mosques of Bradford, where he is now sitting. In *Today's Times,* he has been named and shamed for avoiding massive taxes by setting up companies to pay him, thus avoiding tax, and this is a supposed Left-wing politician?). He went up to Jim Scott and Ned Lynch, asking if he could box. He, however, said he was fit enough and would not need to train, just warm up.

Ned and Jim called myself and Alan Smith over and told us to do a job on him, me first. This guy was six inches taller than me and at least three stone heavier, a real hero when it comes to pushing his weight about. Not that night, though; he came rushing at me, and I hit him with a few solid jabs and my trademark uppercut, then moved out of range. 'Tommy the Toreador' was in control and the angry bull just got a whole lot angrier. He attacked with bravado to the little toreador, and as he threw a left jab, I nicked inside and hit him with the perfect combination of body shots to put the bull on his knees. For the record, I was so happy to see this gabby youth put in his place by a small Lochee tinker who only ever had esteem and relaxed with four posts and three ropes around me! I only add this because, whilst on the *Celebrity Big Brother* show, Mr Brash MP told everyone he had boxed for the Lochee Boys Club, and it makes me mad, knowing his boxing career lasted no more than about three jabs and seven body shots. I got out of the ring, and Alan was getting ready. When Mr MP saw the size, the easiest thing to do without calling him the 'unbrave' word and being sued, as is his way, was to leave Lochee Boys, never to return to the boxing section. Every word is true, and when I heard him on TV saying he had boxed at Lochee Boys Club, I felt the requirement to put that story right.

I had previously won the Army Cadet Force Championship, but honestly had no idea I was above average, as my father would continually berate me when he was present. When I boxed, I would use a cocky move that looked good and then turn looking for applause, only to get clipped by my opponent while looking towards my father; despite winning, I would still get hit by Dad for looking around. Yet all I wanted was my dad to admire my efforts and show some love!

CHAPTER 3

Becoming a Victim

As my boxing progressed, so did my need for some money. I would train three days a week. Then Lochee United FC, who Granny washed the strips for, required two ball boys, and me and my pal Tom Traynor, whose family were on the committee, volunteered. We were soon cleaning boots for the players, making sure the right strip was in place and the boots looked the part.

We also helped Mr Kidd (Dryburgh School janitor), a large amiable man, clean out, fill, and light the huge stove. This was required for hot water, so dirty players could get clean. We were made to feel part of the team, always being included in travel plans to make sure we could be with all the players at the games. One day, we were going to a midweek match at East End Park against East Craigie. I was fitted into the club captain Billy Caswell's car, with Danny McAlpine and Alex Will. We arrived safely and the game kicked off; after fifteen minutes or so, Billy was carried off with a dislocated shoulder.

At half-time, Danny came over and said, 'Bobby! Here is money for the bus, as we don't know what will happen to Billy.' He said to go then, so that I got home before dark. I was leaving the ground and I noticed one of the supporters coming out. I kid you not; he looked like 'Kreacher', the ugliest house elf in Harry Potter novels and films, saying, 'Danny said to help me get home!' We were just talking and passed an old deserted ground in Rodd Road. He said it was steeped in history and was once the ground of a club called St Bernard's. He then said, 'C'mon, I will show you!'

I was not alarmed then and followed him. When we got in the ground, he started speaking about the old changing rooms, saying they were unique.

He kept walking; however, my hackles were raised and I was going nowhere. He came back and asked what was wrong. I said it was dark and dirty. He put his hand into his pocket and pulled out some money and said, 'Come and earn this.'

I, for the very first time in my life, actually panicked and burst out crying, turned quickly, and ran away. I, being very fit, ran away as fast as my legs would carry me, crying incessantly. I passed many, many people on my way to the bus stop on Arbroath Road. Yet not one adult stopped me or asked what was wrong. Yet, in the 1960s, we were a far more caring society. Not one person cared enough as to why I was in floods of tears and obviously upset. I got home and did not tell my dad, as I thought about another hiding. Yet knowing what I know now, I should have done it immediately. That was my first meeting with a paedophile, and it really, really scared me. In fact, it really unsettled me; I withdrew into myself for a week or so. Dad noted it and asked if there was anything wrong with me; of course, I said no, thinking it was trouble. Then Dad said, 'There are an awful lot of bad people out there. If you ever need to speak, come and see me, Son.'

I thought, 'Yeah, right!' But, oh boy, I really wish I had put more faith in my dad. Then I would realise just what a father's role is, instead of trying to make my own version of him.

It was the seven-week summer break, and for most of us, there was never the proposition of a holiday. We instead went berry picking at local farms, from 7 a.m. till 4.30 p.m.; that was 'berry up', time to go weigh in your last amount of berries picked, then run to the top of the field to get the ancient berry buses home. I started like any other youngster picking with an adult, be it your parent, neighbour, or acquaintance. We started at the bottom of the 'dreel' (Dundee term for large row of berries), whilst the adult started at the top, so he could also pick what you missed. The berry fields were great fun; the banter went on the whole day, people shouting the time, telling jokes, having a bit of fun with a girl when older. You never left your berries out of your sight, though, as many people looked to make their money by stealing what you had picked; now, they were scum. It was far too hard-earned to be stolen. If you went to the local farms and picked in buckets, you filled the bucket and squashed berries down, then routinely urinated in the bucket and filled it with more berries (those berries were for dye). When you went to weigh in, it was unusual, because the scales were set at minus six pounds, supposedly the weight of the master bucket used for weighing. There was never a day you did not watch those scales avariciously, watching the man doing the weighing. Me being a fruitcake, I asked him to weigh the master bucket, as it was too much like hard work, picking only to be fiddled when you weighed in. Of course, he told me to f*ck off. What made it worse was that anything which did not weigh exactly was always rounded down a pound, never rounded up; this really cheesed me off!

Funny thing, some of the adults would stop picking about 3 p.m. and play cards for that hard-earned cash. It grew on us all, though, as when I left the forces, the berries were one option of making money. I would pick all day, then get off the bus and go to the bookies, just insane. This is where all the Scots earned their work ethic. Now, the berries are picked by migrants, denying many needy families of much required finance. The farmers go abroad now and sign the migrants to a contract, which does away with 'the minimum wage' and no Scots are allowed this income now. You really could not make this stuff up! Even George Orwell did not see this coming!

When I was seven, I was already a 'wee nabbler', a fast, clean picker who went to make money, not to play half the day, eat all your spam sandwiches in the morning, and go home when bored. I was lucky though, at age eight, Spike Rennie, a fantastic man and a neighbour, was running his own berry bus from Charleston to Blairgowrie via Mid Craigie. The farm we went to was McIntyre's, and the fields were stuffed with heavy produce; if you worked, you could make good money. This saved actually fighting to get on a bus; it really looked to me like the American Depression. Anyone fought everyone to get a day's work! We got on the bus at Charleston without any bother, so long as big Spike trusted you. We then went to Mid Craigie, probably Dundee's toughest, poorest housing scheme then. Danny Sands had his own squad on, just like Spike, however there were guys desperate for a day's work outside the Dundee area, as it was unlikely that social security officers would turn up and catch 'benefit cheats,' thankfully including his daughter, Fiona, who I had an eye for, as we had both grown up on Spike's bus over a period of six to seven years. I got a date with her just palling about at 'the Swannee Ponds', me looking good in a brand new pair of shoes. I took her rowing, making a fool of myself, as I had never rowed before and lost an oar; the upshot was that I went into the water to retrieve the oar and my new shoes got stuck in the mud. She was in stitches. My loose change (bus money home) also disappeared in the pond. I walked four miles home soaking wet and in stocking soles and got another bollocking from Mum; even she saw the funny side though.

I remember the first day I made ten at the berries in 1963. I was over the moon, even though I would have to hand it over to put 'towards the school uniform', the first objective. My mum made me special sandwiches the next day as her way of praise, real ham, not spam. We spent our whole holiday period picking raspberries and strawberries, except when it was raining. These were danger days for me. Working in the fields was great fun. Roaming free was dangerous and normally got me into trouble; you guessed it; I was a pest. Nowadays, they would give me Ritalin for ADHD, however, we will now progress to a sample of those 'Danger Days'!

Paedophile number 2

I was now a four-foot-eleven-inch Scottish champion. There was a man called Thomas Hutchison (pictured). He was station master of a derelict old station called Lochee West, and his job was to close the gates to traffic four times a day manually. I was caught by him stealing lead from the roof, which I would melt down and turn into small ingots, then flog to the scrap merchant Frank Kelbie, a family friend. If you look into the distance of the photo, you will see a small building between two telegraph poles; that was my workshop. Anyway, on getting caught, his methods were sick and condescending. He threatened me with the police, which didn't worry me; they knew me better than I knew myself! Then he threatened me with the line manager, Mr Barr, a lovely neighbour of mine, but who would have reported it to my dad. How sneaky and depraved can things get, you wonder.

He ordered me to be at the station at 11.30 the next day. I arrived and he gave me money and sent me to the shops for biscuits and sweets. I came back, and in this darkened room, there was no electricity, two gas mantles whistled and hissed as he thought, and there was a window which opened for enquiries and a 'line phone' which rang three times to warn of an oncoming train. He gave me his job while he got paid. Then he would ask me personal questions about sex and started showing me indecent pictures, which were nothing by the standards now. He would then feel my crotch and promised he would get girls in and stuff like that. It was seedy, and I had never felt anything like that at any time in my short life. Exciting, yet horrid, suggestive, yet inappropriate, and I knew I didn't like it. He then opened up my trousers and gobbled my penis; it was the most horrid thing ever, yet I ejaculated to my disgust, and he said, 'I knew you were a poof!'

Bastard! He used to sing all the time, as he was a member of the Downfield Musical Society. They were and still are an excellent musical company, who carried out excellent plays and musicals in the city.

Anyway, Hutchison then got a call from Mr Barr, who said he was coming to visit. I was made to hide under the counter and rub his penis while he spoke to my neighbour through the sliding window. I was in revulsion, but Hutchison said that if I didn't do it, then he would bring Mr Barr into the office and I would get a hiding from my dad. After the 'conversation' ended, the 'bastard' went to put on the wooden covers to protect the windows.

It was now very dark apart from the fiery, spitting, hissing gas mantles, and I was scared. He came back in and locked the door; he became furious that I had not satisfied him whilst he was speaking to my neighbour. In a flash, he had me over the comfy chair face down. I was shouting, 'No!' and screaming. As previously stated, I was too small to throw my punches. He stuck his horrid pole up my backside; the pain was immense and I cut my mouth biting the chair. After what seemed an eternity, but was probably forty seconds, he stood up and left me with blood also coming out of my backside. I was going to kill this 'bastard' was my first thought. He then had the audacity to give me a £1 sterling note, a fortune to me with the comment, 'You will return, because you loved it.' I despised every single second of this and never ever went back, despite his threats.

I just tell you this story to protect your own children; there are far more paedophiles now due to the technologies we have. The most important rule I can give as a victim is to always be sure you know exactly what your children are up to. If possible, only use the Internet in one room, so that random paedophiles acting as children are caught quickly.

If I was to catch a paedophile now, I think my answer would be a 50p bullet! I can tell you without fear or favour, it is the most heinous thing that can happen to anyone, male or female. Any self-esteem you may have had disappears. You feel as if someone has ripped out your heart. Within ten minutes, the self-hatred and loathing begins and is a very serious agenda to regain once it has begun.

All I knew was that I was an enraged fighter who had inadvertently become a victim; I was going to fight this every and any way I could. There are wounds that never show on the body, that are deeper and more hurtful than anything that bleeds. We have to live with this, until we are stubborn enough or strong enough to reveal it. Yet revelation to another does not take away the pain and hurt instilled. They say telling someone takes the hurt away. From my point of view, that is not true. I went through more trick cyclists earning good money than you would think. It was only when I was accused of abusing my daughter, I thought 'Whoa!' this has to be resolved. I will resolve it my way!

What is unusual, and all my fault, is that my marraige of thirty years has now died. This is due to my own self-depreciation, which made me very opinionated on the rights and wrongs in this world. We live together to save money but apart in every other way. To me, this hurts just as much as the paedophile day. There is absolutely nothing I can do to retrieve a situation that I induced; all I can say is that I am terribly sorry to my children and my very generous wife, who was a saint putting up with me for so long. Although having stripped the title 'victim' from my back, I find I still have an awful lot to make up for, just to recover my worth as I see it.

Note: About ten years after the events described, my wife and I were travelling to Blairgowrie on a service bus, and a man came up and asked for my autograph; my wife's mouth just opened wide. It was Danny Sands; we talked for a wee while. I think my wife thought I was telling porkies about my boxing career.

CHAPTER 4

The Bullying

In Primary 5-7, we were to get to know a new teacher, Miss Norah Coyle, very well. She helped the achievers achieve; the rest of us were figures of fun! Break times were the only enjoyable time, even though we kicked footballs about and generally played together; being the next thing to a tinker meant you were last to be picked for any team, despite your fitness. I was always picked last and was even a goalpost on cold days, as no one would take their coats off. Imagine how that helped my self-esteem!

Three things stick out from my time in her class: obviously her methods of bullying and picking on the poorest kids comes high on the list, but for me, I was eleven years old perhaps, boxing on a fortnightly basis, training three nights a week, and getting into mischief as we all did, the rest of the time. I was due to box in the Midlands Championships for the first time about March 1966; we were also being taught to swim at the same time. We used to go to the pool twice a week, a fair bus journey and a good laugh normally! We got to the pool and my thigh had some paint on it from the night before—I did not yet have long trousers. We got to the pool and one of the bullies told Coyle about it. I was instantly pounced on and made to stand in the showers rubbing the paint off with carbolic soap for the whole lesson. Let's face it; no way to get gloss paint off, is it? After the forty-five-minute lesson was complete, paint still there (obviously), I got a dose of her 'knuckleduster'; apparently, it was a huge engagement ring. However, I could not see any man going near such a cruel, pernicious, though not unattractive, woman. That wasn't the end of the grief that day. We got back to school, and during the remainder of the day, classmates were getting thumped for watching trains going along the railway line (Yes, the same one!). I am sure it is because of people like her; she is the real reason there is no disciplined alternative in school now.

I was looking out of the window and doing what a lot of children did: I picked my nose and wiped it under the desk; yes, loads of kids did it, still do now. Now remembering I was boxing that night, she opened my desk, made me put my hands inside with my knuckles on the edge, and then slammed the desk down on my hands, leaving them severely reddened. I failed the doctor's medical and could not box.

I mentioned earlier about the trauma I have carried for forty-five years now. During a bright and sunny lunchtime, we were playing a game called king ball. In this game, we all made a circle with legs astride, the tennis ball was bounced in the centre, and whoever's legs the ball went through was 'out' and chased around the playground till they could hit someone else that was playing, with the ball. Anyway, the game was going for around ten minutes when the tennis ball went down the coal cellars, which were open, as they had just been filled, and Bill, the janitor, was doing something else. I, being the smallest and grimiest, was ordered down by the bully to get the ball. As I was re-emerging from the dusty, filthy, gloomy cellar, the said bully ordered a first-term girl (aged five) to release the safety pin and two hundredweight of cast iron landed on my head. I suffered a fractured skull and my eyeball was level with my nostrils. I got out and ran screaming into the school. I was laid on the bed, an ambulance was called, and the three nuns all knelt beside the bed praying and making me feel even worse.

I was a real mess. I had thirty-eight stitches inserted above my left eye and another fourteen in the left-hand side of my head. I also had a suspected fractured skull. Yeah, the bully had done a fine job, but I will not name him for one simple reason: Just last year, my friend Steve Conway and I arranged a fiftieth anniversary night out to commemorate our first day at school. Prior to the event, I had a long talk with the perpetrator, where I told him everything and explained that the week after I left Fifty-nine Commando, I had come across him in the local hospital. I had said, 'Do you know who I am?'

He said, 'Yes', and sneered. It was at that moment I told him that if the place was not so busy, I would have killed him.

We (the bully and I) resolved to meet prior to the reunion and talk it all over. I, being the better man, offered my hand in forgiveness/friendship;

the reunion was brilliant, as there were no wars to fight; I even drove him home afterwards. We even had our original teacher, Sister Mary Angela, in attendance for an hour or so. When she met me outside the club, she said 'Bobby Curran—you taught me the best lesson ever in school.' I asked innocently what that was? Her response still has me giggling, 'Always count the black baby money as soon as you get it!'

Two weeks after the coal bunker incident, our class went to Belmont Camp for a week prior to moving to high school. I was not allowed to go due to the nature of my injury, yet felt I was being punished. I was moved down a year for the time of the camp: It felt like being thumped again, as at that age, you saw them, some only months younger than you, as babies. It is just the thoughts of a child though. Me, I was more worried about boxing again. My mother was so anti-boxing and this could help her cause. I now know my dad, knew he was ill and was trying to make me a man, albeit misguidedly and too early. Dad took me to see a specialist about a month after the incident, and you could have knocked me out when he asked the doctor if I could box again! As the surgeons had done such a wonderful job and made the stitches so close and tight, my doctor said it would be all right to train again and to keep involved, but no sparring until the x-rays got to him.

Things took a lot longer in those days, however the day did come: The skull had no damage other than bruising. This gave me the all-clear to start training and sparring after six more weeks—an eternity to me!

It was probably one of my happiest days, roughly 30 June 1966, the approximate date we left primary school. It was not just the fact that at last we could wear long trousers. It was more to do with having religion stuffed down your throat, no questioning, as previously mentioned, being asked if you were at church that weekend, knowing the belt was just a vestment colour away. The thing I hated most was singing for Sister Mary Ignatious, her chisel-featured, beady, hawk-like eyes hidden behind tinted penny rounder glasses that sat on her tight nose. This Sister took no prisoners and of course forced one to stay behind after 3.45 till she thought everyone 'except me' (the mimer) was doing their very best.

I still see signs of bullying often wherever I go. However, the worst as far as I am concerned occurred in 1993. We had been in our new home for just a few weeks and did not quite realise that children tend to class everyone in a certain way; by that, if a child is intelligent, they are shunned. If the same child has any illness, again this is picked up by the bullies.

Nothing can be done by that child, however hard they try; they will never find favour, as trolls tend to breed trolls, only worse because there is far less discipline now than at any time in history. I was driving back into town and was so happy seeing the children laughing, playing, and generally having fun. I then noticed one child all on her own; within a split second, I realised it was my daughter. I was so angry to see her vilified in such a way; she had done nothing wrong. I immediately drove to the school and took my daughter home in the car. There was no way she was going back to that environment. I called the school and gave the head teacher a difficult time and explained the reason I would not come and enter into dialogue with her! I was in such a rage I would happily have carried out what I saw as reasonable retribution to her assailants' parents; my wife in her good sense stopped this. We immediately called a small village school in Kettins and placed my two younger children there. The difference was astounding. The eldest, however, stayed where she was, as it was only two weeks till she moved up to high school. Despite her difficult time, she was still runner up to the dux.

Unhappily, as I should have remembered, Tina was vilified by the same bullies and others from other schools despite me working full time there. She spent a fair amount of time in hospital through her teen years with an unrelated illness. The head teacher, Mr F, who I despised, had received homework from teachers who knew Tina was very bright. It would take one phone call to the technicians' room, and I would have picked it up and assisted her. He just ignored the homework that had piled up. He was such a poor headmaster that a child was nearly murdered at lunchtime by an enemy with a hammer. I personally feel nothing but contempt for this man, and if he ever reads this, he will know exactly who he is! If ever I see him and I do, I cross the road just to save me from a criminal offence. Some things some of us won't let go.

There was a happy ending despite all the bullying, time off for weeks in hospital, and even teachers saying nasty things out of my earshot. She achieved a psychology degree, is married, and now lives happily in USA.

CHAPTER 5

St John's R. C. Secondary, The Traumatic Years 1966-70

In mid-August 1966, I was introduced to secondary school, and if you thought teachers were bad at primary, I can assure you this lot were sadists in disguise. One funny observation: The cruellest teachers always wore black gowns over their everyday clothing. To be fair, there were some excellent teachers, as well as the usual mix of perverts, gays, sadomasochists. In fact, due to the religious philosophy which was inherited from earlier years—'If in doubt, get the belt out', it was honestly worse than the Army if you moved at break time, when the bell caused you to line up erect and afraid to move. There is absolutely no reason to name any of them apart from the pervert, as most are dead.

In the first year, we came up against stuff we had never done before: woodwork/metalwork/technical drawing/sciences, and we seemed to be expected to know about using tools, etc. However, we muddled along and worked hard together; it was very like a fresh start and we all seemed equal, except that I had three of the St Clement's bullies in my class. I suppose it was a bit like American schools, where the better footballers always got the best, and the St Clements bullies always got that.

In August 1967, I began the second year, not knowing it would be a disastrous, never-to-be-forgotten year at the school. We had two or three excellent teachers in the second year. My favourites were Brother John (geography), Stewart Lilburn (art), Matt McKillen (English), and Head Teacher Brother Bede, who was called 'Pope' behind his back. Anyway, on with the story: On 1 November 1967, nineteen-year-old Robert Mone entered a needlework class taken by Nanette Hanson. He was armed with a shotgun and, for one and a half hours, subjected the teacher and her pupils to a terrifying ordeal. It culminated in the murder of Nanette Hanson. The very first thing I knew was that we heard a bang whilst in Brother John's geography class. He went out of the room, came back in, and right away asked us to keep calm, but that there was a 'madman' in the room next door to ours in the school. We were asked to sit quietly and await further news and say silent prayers. Ten minutes later, the Pope came in and asked us all to very quietly get up and leave the class. We took the first staircase and went out of the school via the back door; it was only then we realised how much danger we could have been in. The back was swarming with armed police! We were instructed to go across the two fields on to the old railway line and to go straight home. I had never met Miss Hanson, but apparently, she was a charming, quiet teacher who was pregnant and she fully made use of great leadership potential: She put the V3 class girls' safety before her own, for which she was awarded the posthumous George Cross for bravery above and beyond what could ever have been expected. We were given three days off school, but to be honest, it was no holiday: Shock and awareness of our luck ensured this, as apparently, he was looking for a Marist Brother or nun or teacher. Robert Francis Mone (born 1948) was a Scottish convicted murderer and spree killer.

Mone was born in Dundee and grew up with his parents and two sisters. He claims to have had a dysfunctional home life and traumatic childhood. In 1964, he was expelled from St John's R. C. High School. He then joined the Gordon Highlanders and served with them in West Germany. He returned to Dundee with depression and began to drink heavily. On 1 November 1967, armed with a shotgun, he entered a girls' needlework class at St John's School and subjected the fourteen to fifteen-year-old pupils and their pregnant teacher, Nanette Hanson, to a one and a half-hour ordeal before shooting Hanson dead and raping one girl and sexually assaulting another. Mone, whose motive was apparently revenge for being expelled from the school three years prior, was found to be insane and sent to the State Hospital for Scotland and Northern Ireland in Carstairs. Mone, of course, made further notoriety by escaping with Thomas McCulloch and killing a nurse, warden, and a policeman in a very short time.

When the school reopened three days later, we had an exorcism Mass to get rid of 'evil', yet to me, it was much like any other Mass! The luck of St John's did not exactly get a lot better, as in September 1968, a young neighbour of mine, Hazel Phinn, twelve, was abducted and murdered by a notorious child killer, who also was sent to Carstairs and died in 2007.

Despite all this, sporting success was always at the school. I played in the goal for the hockey team; we did well, but so many of our football team, bullies included, played for Dundee Schoolboys, and they won many trophies because the coaches within the school wanted winners; a word of praise for the 'teachers'; this was all done voluntarily.

My English was improving rapidly under Mr McKillen, who had a belt called 'Black Bess'. He was Jedburgh House Master, but if you were given the belt, you deserved it and never again committed the same 'crime'. As the other three housemasters were arrogant bullies, I attempted to get involved in music, joining the band. I could read music, no problem; I just could not sing it. I smile now as I remember myself entering the Leng Medal singing competition and coming last. I knew the band never wanted me either; they gave me the tuba. It weighed more than me. I was informed I had to look after it and practice often.

I was dying to show my parents my instrument, so I decided to take it home, however the bus conductor told me the bus was too full for this instrument. I lived 2.8 miles from the school, so there was nothing else for it but to carry this thing home. It took me well over an hour. I'm sure it was the bandmaster's ruse to put me off; it certainly worked. I took the lump of twisted metal back to school and told them it was far too large for me.

Next thing I attempted was the drama group. Now I was always good at drama and was given the lead part of a French tramp (wonder why?)! I thoroughly enjoyed it until some bullies grabbed my bag with the lines in it, ripped it up in front of me, and said, 'We dare you to do something about this.' Red Rag to a bull. I was still tiny and undernourished but went straight to the drama group leader and explained in tears.

He said, 'Do not worry. I got another script. But let me go see to these "idiots".' He followed me to Brother John's class and told the perpetrators to stand up. No one did, so the teacher said, 'That is fine. I will ask Brother John's permission to belt half the class whilst he does the other half!' It took less than five seconds for the three reprobates to stand up; they came back giving me the evil eye, but I did not care. I had kind of lost fear of those people, knowing another thumping was inevitable.

Two final memories from school to tie this episode up was that we were taken to Victoria Cinema as a whole school to see 'The Inn of the Sixth Happiness'—the story of Gladys Aylward, which made a massive impression on me.

The story begins with Aylward being rejected as a potential missionary to China because of her lack of education. Dr Robinson, the senior missionary, feels sorry for her and secures her a position in the home of a veteran explorer with contacts in China. Over the next few months, Aylward saves her money to purchase a ticket, choosing the more dangerous overland route to the east because it is less expensive.

Once in China, she settles in a town, where she secures a post as assistant to a veteran missionary, Jeannie Lawson, who has set up an inn for travelling merchants, where they can get a hot meal and hear stories from the Bible. The film follows Aylward's acculturation, culminating in her taking over the inn when Lawson dies in an accident.

The local mandarin appoints Aylward, a stubborn but endearing woman, as his foot inspector to ensure that the ancient practice of foot binding is eradicated in the region he governs. She succeeds in this and manages to put down a prison revolt as well, winning her the esteem of the local population as well as of the mandarin. Meanwhile, however, Japan invades China and Aylward is encouraged by Lin to leave. She refuses, and as the town of Yang Cheng comes under attack, she finds that she has fifty orphans in her care.

As the population prepares to evacuate the town, the mandarin announces that he is converting to Christianity to honour Aylward and her work (she is rather taken aback by this, as she would have preferred him to convert through religious conviction). She is now left alone with the children, aided by Li, the former leader of the prison revolt that she helped to resolve. Lin tells her that the only hope for safety is to take the children to the next province, where trucks will drive them to safety, but they must get there within three weeks or else the trucks will leave without them.

Just as they are preparing to leave, another fifty orphans appear from a neighbouring town, so Aylward and Li have no choice but to lead one hundred children on a trek across the countryside. Although it should only have taken them a week, the roads are infested with Japanese patrols and the group has no choice but to cut across the mountains. After a long, difficult journey, they all arrive safely (except for Li, who died to save them from a Japanese patrol) on the day the trucks are to leave. Aylward is greeted by Dr Robinson, whom she reminds how he rejected her as a missionary years before.

The film culminates with the column of children, led by Aylward, marching into the town singing the song 'This Old Man' to keep up their spirits. Unusual fact: The film was filmed in Snowdonia using Chinese children from Europe's largest Chinese community, Liverpool. The reason I put this into my autobiography is because this film carried an esoteric message for me. It made me realise that no matter how difficult and downright desperate things can become, we have within us our human spirit and solutions to fight to beat anything.

Towards the end of my time at St John's, I remember a new teacher of geography. I think his name was Mr Rizzio. One afternoon, he called me out for a misdemeanour of some kind. I did not accept his ruling and told him, to the shock of the class, that if he touched me with his belt, I would shove his belt up his backside, all four feet eleven inches of me. So he threw me out of the class, hoping one of the house masters would see me and routinely belt me for misbehaviour. The class lesson bell went and we moved on to English with Matt McKillen. I had a very odd feeling of remorse and asked Mr McKillen if I could go see Mr Rizzio.

He said, 'Do not be long. We have a lot to do!'

I knocked quite timidly on Rizzio's door, and he shouted 'Enter.' He had a class in, and I wasn't facing him with a whole class. I knocked again, and he came out. The look on his face was a picture, as I carefully told him the statement in my head.

'Mr Rizzio, I am so sorry for my behaviour at the last period. I have just had enough of being bullied. However, as part of my apology, I am willing to take your punishment.'

Surprisingly, he offered me his hand and said, 'Robert, today you became a man.'

I shook it and went back to my class relieved. The next Morning at 9.05, I was told to go and see Pope. I knocked on his door as timidly as a field mouse.

He roared, 'Come in!' As he saw me, he opened his right drawer, where I knew his belt was. However, he did not take a belt out; instead, he offered me his right hand, at the same time saying, 'Robert, you have been on my mind since yesterday's incident. I have been thinking and praying what to do. Then, as I drove into school today, the answer came!'

I reached for his outstretched right hand as if to shake it. There was a badge in his hand; it said, 'Prefect'. I was to be in charge of the Admin Block, and my base for breaks and lunch would be in the janitor's room, known there as a Buckie. So people were beginning to see the real me. Pity it was not to last much longer.

The reason I left school was that in September 1970, I sat my Preliminary O Level English and did unexpectedly well, with 100 per cent. On leaving school that day, I was met by the gang of thugs who thought they would teach me the ultimate lesson, giving me another hiding. It was no big deal. I was used to this and many other inane slights whilst at the school.

I did not go back to school; I had just had enough. So for three months, I played truant and helped my uncle rewire houses as his labourer. Those were funny, hilarious times, working for an Asian company rewiring the houses. Then builders would come in and partition it all into small student quarters. It was then fun to have a laugh with Frank (usually at his expense; he was simple to wind up). He gave me a few pounds every week and fed me, so we decided to have a night out to the fun fair. We had a right giggle for all of twenty minutes and went on the 'Octopus', which was an aerial roundabout which kept spinning, all fine and well until the safety pin fell out of the catch. We spent the rest of the ride trying to hold the safety cover on. With this extra exertion, all we could hear was money falling out of Frank's pocket, and he screamed like a child as I giggled in hilarity. I was really happy when this ride finished; firstly, I was safe, and secondly, Frankie lost his money (I was fourteen). Only when I checked my pocket, which was empty, it was my money that went flying. I went to speak to the traveller who ran the ride and demanded he give me my cash back or at least stop the ride till I went and retrieved it.

He said, 'Are you insane? Everything on the ground at my pitch is mine!'

So, I lost my four-foot-eleven-inch temper and hit him very hard to the stomach; one of his mates ran over and escorted me off the site. So Frank was the fortunate one: a job, money, and a girl. I got bus money home. Whooppee!

I knew I had been accepted for the Army Apprentice College, Chepstow, the day after my final school hiding and prepared to embark on the finest years of my life as a proud Royal Engineer.

http://en.wikipedia.org/wiki/Robert_Mone
http://en.wikipedia.org/wiki/The_Inn_of_the_Sixth_Happiness

CHAPTER 6

My Dad, the Family, Life, and Demise

In the first chapter, I talked about my evil dad and his demise. In between times, I have looked again at the possible reasons and consequences of his rages and tempers. He was the younger of three pre-war children, born 21 October 1932. For his formative first five years, he would have had a loving mum and dad (no doubt). His elder brother Tom was a sneak and a bully. His other brother David died at a few weeks old and would have been the eldest born 8 March 1930.

Now from that, take away his loving father, who went to Spain to fight Franco and fascism for two years, came home for three months, then was in the first batch of volunteers to fight Hitler. He was an amazing man in my opinion, because had it not been for the depletion of the Spanish troops, there is no doubt they would have been with Adolf Hitler and Mussolini during the war. The strength of that Army, in my opinion, would have won World War II. However, as history showed, Spain became a neutral country during World War II, as dictator General Franco did not have enough resources to assist his friends Hitler and Mussolini and had no option but to join the Swiss as neutral, though checking history, Spain was really a rest and recuperation area for his allies armies.

So let's look at Robert Curran for a few minutes: bullied by his bigger brother, his mother so busy trying to make ends meet, working all day, then going home to make the evening meal, worried not just about her children, but also her beloved husband and what he was doing, no doubt spilling her aching heart in the few occasional letters. That apart, she had no one really to release to. Not only were they mistreated by the Catholic priests because their father was apparently a 'Communist traitor, against the

Church of Rome', when Rab needed the guiding influence of a good man, there were none, as most of them were off to war. He was quite obviously a very intelligent boy, as he did well at school and became a chief engineer in the merchant navy immediately after his National Service 1951-53. Can you see what is happening here? I no longer blame my dad for anything. In fact, I wish fervently I had confided more in him instead of living in fear. He obviously had no guiding influence in the formative years, and Granny Lizzie, a tough but tiny Glaswegian, couldn't hurt two teenagers roughly five feet nine inches tall.

My other grandparents were Adam McKay McConnachie and Mary, who I have already mentioned. Addie was a tower crane driver; Mary was always happy and relaxed when he was away working on major constructions, such as Pitlochry Dam and a few shopping centres. However, whenever he had a local job, such as the Tay Road Bridge and the Wellgate Centre Dundee, he would finish work, go home, and immediately berate Mary, whether it was her cooking or she had not bought enough alcohol. He was a 'party animal' who used to think he was the life and soul of the party, playing his Louis Armstrong songs on his piano and with loads of 'friends' drinking his alcohol and laughing and joking. For me and Frank, my uncle who is five years older than me, it was great for collecting money. One night, Frank and I went to bed and had our achievement of coins stacked on bedside tables; I was jealous that his was double mine. So next morning, I woke early, got dressed, and pocketed mine and Frank's. I sneaked down the stairs silently (I thought!), opened, and closed the door with my pirated treasure trove in my pocket. I had not got to No. 19 when Frank came flying out of 21 dressed in underpants and he chased me down Dryburgh Crescent, catching me within 150 yards, thumped me deservedly, took all the cash back, but kindly gave me mine back. He kicked my arse with his bare feet and said, 'Beat it or I will really batter you!' (He could not fight sleep on a good day, LOL.)

To be fair, though, Addie and Mary looked after my great-grandmother, Mary Chalmers, for well over fifteen years; they slept on a bed settee to give my great-grandmother a room for herself. She had her own call system, a walking stick banging on the floor until someone went to her service. Every Saturday, I used to be summoned to go shopping for her quarter-pound pat of butter and her 'Crawford's Water Biscuits!' When parties or New Year's or birthday celebrations were on, she would get herself sat in the living room as the matriarch 'Queen Bee'. Once she was drunk, it took a while; she had to be put to bed. In her final years, she was five feet high and three feet wide and actually reminded me of HRH Queen Victoria. Frank and I were requested to put her to bed. We managed to get her to the foot of the sixteen stairs; then the fun began. She would be shouting/singing, 'More Vodjika,' and Frank and I would have a shoulder blade and a bum cheek, pushing the dear old lady up the stairs. We felt like removal men, but it was hilarious then and just as funny now. Her brother-in-law was James Chalmers, who invented the sticky postage stamp.

I must digress, as I have always wondered where the tumour that killed Dad came from. The story that I was told was that he was drunk and walked out in front of a car outside 'The Whip Inn' (a local hostelry), stood up, and got a bus home, refusing any type of medical check over. My theory is much more obvious, as I witnessed this.

Mum and Dad had their usual Friday night imbibing session and incumbent war after 10 p.m.: Closing time in those days. They came home arguing. Dad threw a punch and broke Mum's nose, so it was two kids up (me and Valerie, the youngest) and on the trip to Dryburgh to McConnachie house. Addie, who was a big bully himself, whom I shall come back to, was shouting and swearing, 'Gonna kill Rab, etc.' There was only one problem . . . he was sober, not brave enough. Anyway, we go to sleep for a few hours, have breakfast, and went back to 25 Craigmount Road. Dad immediately apologised and was just being busy, trying to make up for his drunken aberration. At about 6 p.m., I saw my grandfather, Addie, coming down the road looking like thunder; he was drunk and therefore brave. He passed me and said he was going to kill my dad! Well I was still small, eleven years old, I think, but I knew the look and ran straight to the phone box and phoned the police. I ran frantically home to make sure my dad was OK. I was met by a black and blue 'Elephant Man'. Dad was lying on the couch and at no time defended himself. As far as he was concerned, he made an error; this was family retribution. I have never in my life, even up to now, seen anybody whose face was in such a mess. The police came, Dad said it was a personal matter, and it was just left there. I have only thought over the last few months that, in effect, my grandfather killed my dad.

Dad died at 4.30 on 20 July 1969 in Victoria Hospital, which is the place of no return in Dundee. I remember the time clearly because our dog, Shane, started the most curious howling at 4.30 a.m. At 5 a.m., there was a knock on the door by the police telling Mum of Dad's death. We were told on waking up, and all of us cried despite some of the things that had been done.

The Funeral

My mother refused to let any of the children go. I argued and swore, but she was adamant. I was not getting to say goodbye! I was to look after the other three siblings till she got back. Anyway, we really did not have clothes suitable for church. I read the paper to get the timings of the church and rrematorium. I asked my wee brother Tam to watch the girls, and at 9.50, I was hiding beside the post box watching the hearse bringing Dad into church, weeping furiously. Once everyone was in church, I ran 800 metres and stood outside 'The Rowantree', another passing place of the Cortege. I remember seeing the hearse coming up the hill, and I stood to attention crying. My grannies were in the same hearse, saw me, and started crying as well. The whole lot came back to our house for the wake afterwards, and both of them grabbed me and cuddled me for life itself. I rebelled against my mum because of her decision and was sent to live with my uncle Frank for a week till I calmed down. Frank said he would help sort me out; I found that funny, as Frank, my favourite uncle, was just slightly older than me and really did not have a bad side to him in any way.

I was then an Army cadet, and my dad had spent hours teaching me to bull boots and how to iron old battledress effectively. I even won the Part 1 competition between seventy youngsters in drill turnout, map reading, and fieldcraft. This normally meant you got promoted. There were only two merits awarded, one to Lance Corporal Albert Hannan and the other to Still Cadet Gunner Curran, a 'dropshort' to be fair, though there was no engineer unit in Dundee.

As the annual cadet camp was always during the Dundee Holiday Fortnight (last week July, first week of August), everyone thought it would do me good. So off I went to Penicuik Camp near Edinburgh with my 'mates' going to be looking out for me (yeah right). The first night there, one of the much older but immature young men thought it would be fun to masturbate over the top of me; the room was in stitches with laughter and I will never ever forget my scream, 'I want my dad!' On my very first leave from A. A. C. Chepstow, I sorted this clown out and felt extremely proud of myself. The guys there had given me back my hidden gift of 'self-esteem'; no one was taking that away from me from then on hopefully. So *Dad*, from me to you, _Respect: R.I.P Robert Curran 21 October 1932-20 July 1969_

CHAPTER 7

Chepstow—the Happy Years—Section 1

So there I was, on 5 January 1971, at 8.30 p.m., standing on Platform 1 of Dundee Tay Bridge Station to meet the recruiting sergeant major, receive my rail warrant, and meet a few other victims. The Army had booked us a six-seat cubicle; whilst most of the guys had bags, stereos, food, etc., I had a small suitcase with all my worldly belongings and one treasure stowed within it. Those where my white kangaroo skin boxing boots, which I earned by guising/busking. Remember, I was tone deaf and the Lochee ladies in the bingo queue paid up so that I would go away. There was a hint of trepidation and excitement for us all. I had only ever been on a train once: to my first Army cadet camp at Bellerby in Yorkshire two years previous, but never an all-night journey!

    I cannot for the life of me remember anyone's name except Ian Grant from Perth on our first expedition together, but there were loads of laughs for about two hours. At that point, we were exhausted, as we had never been up past midnight very often, except in my case to traipse the streets with one parent or the other. Trying to work out how to sleep, you could see we were going to be Royal Engineers. We took all the cases from the roof racks and laid them as level as possible on the floor. I tried to sleep on one of the luggage racks, as did another light soldier, two guys lay horizontally on the couch-type chairs, Ian lay on the floor with the luggage, and one guy sat near the door with his feet stretched across the passageway. It was fine for thirty minutes until the conductor came in to check our rail warrants. He just went berserk, telling us he would give us five minutes to have everything back to normal or we would be booted off the train at the next stop: York. We immediately put everything back the way it should be. We were shit scared of getting into more trouble. You have to remember we were fifteen years and four months old, as an average. Anyway, we just started telling each other about ourselves: what we did for fun and the usual dismal stuff!

I just mentioned I was Scottish 6st 7lb Junior Boxing Champion and none of the obvious poor stuff. We then arrived at Birmingham New Street Station, where we had to change to another platform for the Cardiff train which would stop at Chepstow. I had never ever seen anything like that, a massive station with escalators and shops all over the place. In fact, I had never seen an escalator, so I had a wee bit of fun running up the down escalator and getting abuse in a really unusual accent.

To me, though, it was an adventure. On the Cardiff train, we saw places I had only ever heard about, the River Severn, and an even bigger, better bridge than our own Tay Road Bridge, Worcester, Cheltenham, which I knew of because of my dad's gambling habit. The downs were beautiful. I always thought England was a dump, but in my time down there, that was soon re-evaluated.

Then we heard the conductor say, 'The next stop will be Chepstow.' Excitement and lots of trepidation of the unknown set in. We did not have to worry about fear for long, because there on Platform 1 of Chepstow

Station—there were only two platforms—was this thick-set, hairy-arsed, big-mouthed sergeant who was from C Wing called Sgt Cox and his terrier dog nipping at our heels.

He roared, 'Get your arses on that bus *now*!' Honestly, I have never seen twenty guys (more joined the initial six at York, Crewe, and Birmingham) embark on a bus with luggage faster in my life! It was a clapped-out old Army green bus, where the diesel felt like it wafted inside and made you feel sickly. Through Chepstow was a three-minute job, except for viewing a magnificent ruined castle at Chepstow, then over the beautiful River Wye, up a long hill, and a turn right into Sedbury. As we left Sedbury, we could see the Severn Bridge before us in all its beauty, never realising how well a few of us would get to know this bridge! Then we drove into Beachley Camp with Sergeant Cox shouting out directions of where things were and what we would be doing, but it all went over our heads. We were dropped off in J for Junior Company block and dissipated to our allotted wing. I was in B Wing. There were three floors. On each landing, there were six single rooms for NCOs and beds in blocks of sixteen beds in an open-plan double room. At each end of the corridor were thirty-two beds in total, enough for the whole platoon.

In the very centre of the layout, there was a TV room with a large colour TV; I thought I had died and gone to heaven! Even better, there was no meter on the back. There were three rows of fairly comfy armchairs and a toilet block at each side of the TV room. We were the first of the day's intake to arrive and were quickly made to run to the stores and collect all our kit, including mattress, pillows, and bedding, in rapid time. I was knackered; remember, I wasn't even five feet tall yet. Then we heard some of the senior lads coming in to take the piss and tell us we were *pigs* and would wear pigsuits (coveralls) for the first six weeks. I said, 'I am nobody's fucking pig!'

They all burst out laughing and explained we were called 'PIGS', as we were the new group coming in and P. I. G. stood for Passing In Group and everyone had been through it. It was 11.45 and our Platoon Sergeant Dave Williams came and took us to the cookhouse for dinner, to show us what was where, and help us to get established. We walked round the corner and I couldn't believe my eyes: The cookhouse did not serve one meal at each lunch, but a choice of sixteen different options in four queues. We were in first and fed before the college got up for dinner and had a fantastic choice. It was Christmas, birthdays, and Easter all rolled into one! Magic! Yet being an athlete, I was ever mindful of my weight per height ratio for boxing. We were told we would be free but would have a platoon brief by Sgt Williams at 18.30, when everyone would be in the platoon accommodation.

We got to know each other bantering, laughing, and joking and were brought over to the NAAFI to meet the WRVS lady—Mavis, who showed us the facilities we could use and what we could not use as first-termers. Then at 16.45, I had my very first fight. I was queuing for tea and this tall skinny guy with a red badge (A Company) behind his cap badge (Cpl Pickersgill) walked past me in the queue. I thought that would be right and grabbed him and asked where he was going.

He just said, 'You will learn, Piggy.'

Without a second thought, I threw a left hook to his chin and he staggered. Then he came and ripped into me (learning curve). I went back to my room after eating and promptly fell asleep. Sgt Williams, a really nice guy, just promoted, called the room together at 18.30. I however was in an unconscious state, having been up all night and never having eaten quantities of food like that. I was woken but fell back to sleep; anyway being woken, I was aware I required the toilet, so I walked past the platoon, went to the toilet, and walked back to bed. Sergeant Williams shouted, 'Curran, get your arse over here now!' to which my reply was:

'Fuck off,' and I went back to sleep. I could only imagine what the rest of the platoon thought.

When I woke next, it was 7 January at 6 a.m. As the aforementioned Duty Sergeant Cox used to come into the room, put the lights on, and shout, 'Terrier Alert!', if you never moved, his terrier was put in the bottom of your bed! I promise, you would be out of bed like a rabbit being chased by a weasel. We were then taught to wash and shave properly and clean our teeth. Everything was taught like we were children, which was appropriate: I didn't even have a razor, as I had no sign of pubic hair, never mind bum fluff, but shave I had to, regardless.

Sergeant Williams came in and shouted, 'Curran, my office now!' So I went into his room and stood at attention; remember, I was an Army cadet. He said, 'What have you got to say for yourself, lad?'

I replied, 'I am 24218361 Apprentice Tradesman Curran.'

He said, 'Well done, but about yesterday's insolent behaviour!'

I said, 'Sergeant Williams, I can only apologise. I have never ever been up forty-eight hours without sleep before.'

He smiled and said, 'I hear you are handy with your fists?' Somebody obviously reported my cookhouse attempt!

I said, 'I am trained in the art of boxing, Sergeant.'

That evening, Sergeant Williams took me up to the old gym at the Beachley exit gate, where I met an old man called Tommy Slaven. I say old man; he must have been sixty but was so fit; he was a civilian member of the physical training staff.

They were obviously expecting me, as there where loads of people in the gym: judo players, senior NCOs, and older apprentices. I was told to glove up. I put on my only valuable things: my white boxing boots and black silk shorts, gloved up, and went into the ring. Tommy said, 'This is your test, to see if you are good enough for my team.' They had a different boxer in each corner, who, unbeknown to me at the time, were either Army junior champions or Midlands Army District champions. Yes, they were prepared OK. This may sound big-headed, and it may well be, but for two one-minutes-thirty-second rounds and one two-minute round, I took over the ring; none of the champions could lay a glove on me whilst I was hitting them fairly easily. Mick Blomquist, who became a good friend, was then first Army champion and I was six stone five pounds maximum; he was actually shouting, 'Stand still, you little shit, so I can hit you!' Not bloody likely. As I left the ring, I received a round of applause, which told me I had arrived!

Tommy was a man who treated me as the 'Special One'. He arranged many bouts for me in my twenty-seven months at Chepstow. Each and every time, he would take me to his home about 4 p.m., give me a light meal like scrambled eggs, told me to relax, then we would leave about 7 p.m. for the boxing venue. He actually made me feel exceedingly special, then would gain revenge by beasting me at our platoon's next PT session.

CHAPTER 8

Chepstow the Happy Years—Section 2

Ask anyone who has had experiences at Chepstow: After they have concluded, each and every one will tell you, 'It was the making of *me!*' It had so many wonderful happy memories, alongside the 'beastings' and visits to 'Daktari': Doctor Colonel Taylor (Rtd.). So where do we start? Simple, right at the very beginning! We woke up on Day 3, with our very first bed-and-locker inspection from Sgt Williams R.E. We thought we were wonderful, having made what we thought was the 'identical creation' of the beautiful bed layout and locker inspection layout shown us on Day 2 by JD and Eggs, our two apprentice corporals. Oh, how proud was I of my first locker! It was just amazing; everything laid out as per the diagram that was left to help us. Yes, pride comes before a fall. In my case, the window was opened and I, standing to attention, could hear the noise of stuff falling from the first floor on to J Company's square. Sgt Williams screamed at me, 'Go look out the window!'

I said, 'Yes, Sergeant.'

Looking out the window, I saw every piece of equipment I had signed for two days earlier. I got quite emotional and cried once I had got downstairs to retrieve the equipment, part by part. I eventually got everything back to my bed space and was told to leave it on the bed, as we had an appointment with 'Daktari', our supposed doctor, and that everything would have to be back in my locker 'correctly' by 18.00 hours. This was for the second inspection for the whole room, as it wasn't just my equipment that did the flying trick.

We were then formed up and marched like the penguins parade at Edinburgh Zoo, arms and legs all over the place, berets which looked like bin lids, and shirt, KF itchy, and coveralls, the 'pig suit', over the 300 yards to the medical centre to get our first inoculations/health check/blood check.

The apprentices always called him 'Daktari' because, apparently, he was an animal vet. Certainly the way he treated me, through my seven terms, he must have been a vet, because I sure felt like a poor animal in his presence. The routine was simple. Everyone dropped coveralls to the waist and then rolled up a shirt sleeve. We then lined up in alphabetical order and queued along the medical centre corridor. Hearing the word 'Next!', you ran into the room, jumped on to the scales, weight shouted out by one of Daktari's assistants, height taken by another assistant, then was body pinched for thickness of skin (now known as BMI, body-mass index).

I stepped forward one step and there was the big bald old duffer (the kindest I can possibly be about him) with a trolley beside him and a stethoscope in his ears. First, it was three deep breaths, and then it was the right arm on waist, first inoculation. He then sliced everybody's right ear and took a blood sample into small bottles which were prepared in order, previously. He would then hand you a bit of cotton wool to stem the torrent of blood from the right ear. The shout went up, 'Next!', and you were out of the room and told to run back to the block; that was simple. You just followed the trail of apprentice blood! We wondered what had hit us. We got to the block, and about an hour later, the blood was staunched and we got on with 'room recovery': refolding shirts, sheets, and bed blocks. There were times prior to inspections that we actually slept on the floor to keep everything pristine, or at least our idea of pristine.

Eggs came back in to our side of the accommodation, whilst JD went to the other end, and they assisted us and gave us great tips for future survival, showing us places the 'CSM' (who?) would be checking that night. What made us feel even better was our company sergeant major, CSM Phil Langley, one of the greatest men I have ever met. He was a stickler for discipline, as I would find out four days later, but passionately cared about each and every young man in his care.

At 18.00 hours, 'Stand by your bed!' was shouted, and in strutted this big, bad, ugly CSM, who was really more interested in looking for dust in odd places and giving you grief and taking the piss without being out-and-out nasty.

The floor was polished and his tackety best boots were scuffing the floor (We spent hours buffing our floors with heavy manual bumpers or buffers). Again, I felt near to tears! Anyway, after inspection was finished, he got both rooms together and told us just how awful we were, then told us not to worry. He was sure that within six weeks, each of us would be ready and prepared for the Passing-in Parade, which was when we would get our first weekend leave. Then, we would be allowed out of camp on trips to Bristol with Mavis (WRVS), etc. We would also be allowed to go to the disco on Saturday nights, when local girls came to 'check us out'. The truth was that none of the girls were interested in J Company lads unless they were a wee bit older, which is how Frank Hall always scored when not in 'the nick'. He had a lovely girlfriend called Gaynor Hopkins. How could such a bonny girl go with 'Irish'? I am still trying to work that one out! Anyway, CSM Langley then stood up and smiled, then shouted to our two apprentice corporals, 'Half hour quick change, Gentlemen!'

Without a doubt, my funniest memories were the 'quick change parades'. You were told what to wear and then had to run outside, within perhaps three minutes, looking absolutely ludicrous with the bizarre combinations of army equipment that were put together, e.g.:

1) Long johns, respirators, and steel helmets
2) Pyjama bottoms and greatcoats
3) PT kit and best boots

You can see that although it was fast and degrading, it was also highly hilarious, especially for 70c Group, who would be on the top floor and you could hear them whistling out of the windows and taking the piss. Yes, this was going to be fun!

Day 4: We started intensive drill skills with Sergeant Williams and were often threatened with no smoke breaks (for the few) or extra drill at night to ensure you concentrated on what was being taught. We were getting there, and a lot of fun and bonding took place. I remember the guys used to use the centre of our room as an imaginary boxing ring where they would try and tag me (no punching allowed) and they used to give up after a few minutes of pit-a-pat taps from me. I, though, just loved the showing off. I seemed to crave attention, which was obviously due to the lack of it to that point.

Day 6: On block jobs and litter clearing, one week into training, I refused to pick up a fag butt despite being ordered three times: I was on my first charge, known as a 252. I was, within hours, standing outside CSM Langley's office being screamed at, marched down to the office of the officer commanding (OC), Major Field, a name I was going get to know, and who had a bearing even at the end of my career! The CSM marched me in at rapid time, and Corporal Adams, who charged me, was there as a witness.

I was crapping myself. The 252 charge was read out, and I was asked if I was guilty or not guilty.

I replied, 'Not guilty.' The room atmosphere suddenly changed. Eggs proceeded to give his truthful evidence and was dismissed.

Then Major Fields said, 'You have heard the evidence. Why did you not obey the order?'

I said, 'Well, sir, I have never smoked and find the thought of picking it up obnoxious!'

There was laughter from the OC and the CSM. 'Do you drink Coke, Curran?'

'No, sir.'

The OC was getting angry. 'Eat sweets?'

'No, sir, I watch my weight!'

He then did not have anything to think of and said, 'If your friend dropped his money, would you pick it up and return it?'

I said, 'Yes, sir,'

'Guilty! Three days Restriction of Privileges (ROPs). March him out, Sergeant Major.'

I was duly marched out and Langley berated me, but I could see he had found it funny; nevertheless, he made me run to the guardroom with the following statement in my head: 'Staff, I am 24218361 A/T Curran and have just been sentenced to three days ROP for disobeying a direct order.' I then tasted my first military 'beasting' from Regimental Police Sergeant 'Barsteward', who gave me a life-shattering verbal assault and, of course, my three days' ROP. These were the dirtiest possible jobs: scrubbing kitchen side floors in the mess hall, clearing the old incinerator area, even picking up used condoms (had never seen one before) from out back of the Naafi on Sunday. Suffice to say, I picked up anything and everything ever since, but still managed a good few charges and did plenty of restrictions, mostly caused by my big mouth; I have not as yet learnt to curb that.

We had been introduced to the gymnasium twice already, and everyone always worried what was in store. We were never let down. Bombardier Gordon, a big amiable black man, Corporal Mick O'Shaugnessy, Irish Fusiliers, and Tommy Slaven used to put us through hell for forty minutes, but we were mostly fit, and I certainly felt no pain after a gymnasium session, although a few did. After Day 4's PT session, I was called to the PTI's door and was informed that I had made the boxing team and given time off for training 'compulsory' as had been agreed with Platoon Sergeant and CSM Langley. Though I would have to pull my finger out, as I was boxing in the

Western District Championships in a fortnight! I was also disqualified from first-term boxing championships.

I was then forced to go for a long boxing medical with 'Daktari' to get my medical book signed; he took over twenty minutes, making me stare into lights without moving my eyes and hundreds of other things that had never been in any medical I had ever had as a boxer. He was very impatient and scathing at my BMI; however, he signed me fit. Guys in the room were miffed, as it was 'preferential treatment': me going training whilst they were block cleaning. Corporal Eggs Adams would take my best boots away and work on them for me whilst I went and made myself fitter, stronger, faster. Apart from my boxing, I also played in goal for the college from first term; this was unheard of and, as I had taken Corporal Pickersgill's position, I had officially made an enemy.

In Week 3, as our drill and room tasks were really improving, we felt like a team. We then started our trade training and education, two days a week of each. I was to be the Army's worst ever electrician, as I thought I knew it all due to my four months of truant, working as my uncle Frank's apprentice. Our tutor was a civilian, Mr Charlie Chase. We never saw eye to eye. I soon realised I didn't want to be a 'Sparkie', but knew not how to get out of it! For example, in the first term, it was all theory except for wiring a plug!

Nevertheless, Week 3 was my landmark: I went to Oswestry with the rest of the boxing team for the Western Championships: my first time out of camp; the team did well there. I had three bouts in two days, winning all comfortably and becoming the first champion of the year, as my weight was the lightest possible.

Going back to Chepstow, I realised just how lucky we were, because to me, Oswestry was like Belsen Camp compared to our 'Hilton Hotel'. Nevertheless, there was no time to be praised, just get back and catch up with everyone else. We worked hard at all the individual Army fitness tests and apprentice expectation tests: a mile in five minutes thirty seconds. This was my first angry moment at Chepstow. The whole platoon took their mark and the gun was fired. I went out moderately fast but well within myself; on the last lap, I lapped a great guy from Motherwell, Matty Mathieson, and smiled as I passed him, obviously well within the time. After he had finished, having missed the time, Matty told the PT staff that I had only ran three laps. Bombardier Gordon then failed me, and I burst out crying in an 'anger rage'. I was made to come back the following week, in my own time, with the other 'fails' to run it again. This time, still raging, I went out fast and stayed in front the whole way for a time of four minutes forty-nine seconds. Bombardier Gordon, I think, knew, but to keep the morale of everyone up, said, 'Curran, that is how you should have run it the first time!'

We then spent the last week of those first six weeks trying on our newly tailored No.2 dress and peaked cap and going through Passing-in Parade rehearsals, preparing for our long weekend off. I was going home!

Thursday, 18 February, 11 a.m.: We were marched on to the Regiment Drill Square looking the part, feeling the pride, the hackles on the back of your neck were raised with an intensity I had never felt before. I saw many parents who lived nearer watching with wonder at the difference six short weeks had made in many of our lives. In the last week of first term was held the finals of the Junior Apprentice Boxing, and although I was barred, I wasn't getting off lightly. I was going to be boxing an exhibition.

'No big deal' said I.

Anyway, the night came and after B wing took the boxing cup, I was gloved up ready to go. I possibly was in oblivion mode, having rested on the pool diving board (my chill area) because, for three rounds, I took the skills literally out of this talented civvy and turned them all to my advantage. We were given an amazing round of applause. It was only then, I learnt, I had just given a boxing lesson to 1970's Junior ABA Runner-up! It just felt so easy, and really, with my relaxation programme, I felt at the time I could beat any light flyweight in the country. The ring was the only place I really felt of worth.

CHAPTER 9

Chepstow, the Happy Years—Section 3

Well, after coming back from our first leave, I had new jeans (cheapest available) and Eggs Adams burst out laughing and tried to tell me about style. Anyway, Eggs actually went and from his own pocket, bought me a pair of smart jeans so I would not look daft; yet I did not feel daft.

As previously explained, I had to go on sick parade, which meant I had to see Daktari, second day back from leave. I woke up and just could not speak. Anyway, the long and short was a visit to Tidworth Military Hospital to see a specialist and being ordered to have two weeks in the Medical Reception Station with Streptomycin injections every two days, without doubt, the sorest injections ever; I think he must have deliberately blunted the needles. Of course, whilst in the MRS, you are a victim to the yeast extract and cod liver oil. I knew yeast extract would add weight and bulk that I did not want, so I used to swallow that and the cod liver oil and then, within two minutes of the Gestapo leaving the ward, I would go to the toilets and make myself sick (the original bulimic).

Older guys who had girlfriends were allowed private visits with screens round the bed. Then, when they left, you would see big cheesy grins and the stories of sticky fingers and everything else behind the screen; by heck, I was jealous!

Eventually, I got out of the MRS with my voice intact and then just went back to boring trade training and laughs in the education block. There were only four weeks of first term left and Charlie Chase decided I would be put back a term due to my illness. I was still remarkably very fit, and in Week 11 of the first term, I travelled back to Oswestry for the Army Championships, despite Daktari's misgivings. I weighed exactly 6st 7lb on the button and met some exceptional boxers there, who were to later join me in the Army team. Not to bore you, I again won the title convincingly. To get the detail out of the way, I had a total of fifty-one military fights. I only lost two, one of which was sheer theft at Chepstow and funnily enough happened to assist my second sport. Att least, that is what I am saying and sticking to!

So there I was, back at Chepstow, knowing I was going to be a PIG again and was really pissed about it. I went on spring leave for two weeks; nothing much happened except a few fights with the school bullies, only I didn't back down. I had stretched three inches and two foot sizes in only thirteen weeks. Sapper Yates, who was the J Company store man, was really annoyed with regularly changing my equipment; you would think it was his money and my fault!

I got back to camp early as I hated being on leave and thumbed it down to London so I could have a few days in the city before I went back to Chepstow. I got picked up near Stirling and was driven to Gretna; it would have been a good deal further, but the guy 'tried it on' with 'pretty boy' Curran. I warned him that as Army champion, I would break his nose. It must have sounded funny, as I was all of five feet two inches tall. He grabbed me, and the buttons on my shirt were torn off. He had, of course, stopped the car, but not to be outdone, I head-butted him, drawing blood, and told him to give me the time to get my case out the car or I would inform the police. I got my case and was left with a mouthful of exhaust smoke as he drove swiftly away.

I went into, as was then, the Gretna Transport Café. One of the drivers seeing my shirt asked what happened. After my explanation, he immediately bought me some food, then went out to his CB radio and asked any of his company's drivers going south to pick up a young soldier and take him onwards to London. Within an hour, I was on my way south and dropped off at Trafalgar Square. Gentlemen, I now salute you. Thank you.

I was then in London; bloody hell, did I feel overwhelmed! I could read maps obviously but had never seen anything like the London Tube system. An older guy said 'Can I help you?' I said I wanted to go to the Army Navy Club, not knowing boy soldiers were not allowed on premises. He took my bag, and when I was refused, he said, 'You can stay at my place for a few days!' My hackles raised again, so I said I had to go to an Army recruiting office as ordered. He dropped my bag and walked away. I did just that: went to a recruiting office and explained my situation, and after fifteen minutes, a Land Rover picked me up and took me to a guards barracks in London.

There, I was given a bed and meals for the day and a travel warrant to go back to Chepstow!

I got back a day before everyone else, and CSM Langley was waiting and gave me what for. However, he was very understanding as well. I was told the travel warrant would be taken off my annual allowance, then told me, 'I am glad you are safe, you silly, naive f****r!'

Everyone was back the next day, and 71A moved upstairs. I was told to stay in my own bed, but to join the potential apprentices from last term for the first six weeks, as we were soldiers and would not be beasted! Phew! That was a relief! I had worried about that. Anyway, the pot-apps were all exactly like me, either awaiting a space on chosen course, which did not run every term, or trying to ensure they were first on the list for courses which were all oversubscribed.

Those six weeks were a joy for everyone of 'Back Squaded Troop': We learnt great soldiering skills under four permanent staff sergeants. We were taken to the Forest of Dean for a week and given tasks to do. We were split into four groups (I led one) and told we would take turns at guarding camp, etc. We were also informed that at the end of the week, we would be doing a ten-mile forced march, except the winning group of six. I nearly blew it at the very start, as the boss knew I would. I said, 'Sergeant, not being funny, but we have a cook (Slop Jockey) with us, so there must be food!' Anyway, after my usual big-mouth moment, our cook came over; he was short, squat, ginger, broken-nosed, and from Manchester with a delightful sense of humour! He ruffled my hair and said, 'Go get me something decent to cook or it is compo rations.'

Firstly, we had to leave camp and bring back food for our evening meal without stealing and avoiding our training staff. We left at 10.00 hours and had to be back at 16.30. I got my group together, pointed at the map, and said, 'Right, guys. Let's go to this secluded farm and ask if they have any work for us!' It was not breaking the rules, and we wouldn't get caught. All agreed without exception. We walked very carefully to our objective, at one point sitting in a dry culvert with the training staff Land Rover above us. They were talking loudly and perhaps, knowing we were there, doing a bit of baiting. I, for once, kept my mouth shut. They were there about ten minutes, but from our point of view, it could have been an hour; time really does become static. We eventually reached our objective, and with fingers and toes crossed, I knocked on the farmer's door, told him our assignment, and asked if we could assist him in any way. A huge smile appeared on his face, and he brought us into his walled front garden: It was like a corn field. He said, 'Can you cut this, lads? I have all the tools.'

We looked at each other, and I said, 'Yes, no problem!'

Firstly, he taught us how to use a sickle, and all six of us got stuck in and cut the grass down to about four inches. We then got two lawnmowers and cut the grass, then rolled it. We even collected the long grass and tied it in bundles. Exaggeration is not nice, but to me, it looked like Wembley Stadium. The farmer came into the garden and the look on his face was magical, gratitude personified. He asked if we would like a drink and brought loads of tins of soft drinks, sandwiches, and crisps out, and we sat and chatted whilst his wife prepared the raw food we had to bring back! Twenty minutes later, at 16.00, we left with four huge carrier bags full of everything from Steak, Milk, Tomatoes to Coke. We knew we had done well and 'strutted' into camp. The cook was completely overwhelmed, but there was plenty for all thirty, including the permanent staff! I had never in my life known charitable country folk, as I only ever went to the Berries. However, I just thought this couple were fantastic, when really all we had done was a large Bob-a-job task.

Another group came in (riding a bloody horse!) with a chicken, obviously nicked, but they were given an axe to chop its head off and told to prepare it for cooking. They cut the chicken's head off and the damned thing actually ran along the table before falling over. They were forced to take the horse back and make an excuse to the farmer; I would have loved to be a fly on that wall, although knowing who the perpetrator was, he could sell sand to the Saudi Arabians.

The sergeant in charge was a huge Sherwood Forrester; his name will never escape me: Sgt Big! He told my group that, as a result of our win, we were going to guard the camp that night (some bloody privilege) whilst the permanent staff went out and then warned us of a gypsy camp who would steal our equipment. As soon as it was dark, everyone except my section—the guard (and permanent staff out on the piss), was asleep. Less than forty-five minutes later, we heard a vehicle stop, but a good way off.

Then stones were thrown at us, noises were made, and I was crapping bricks. Using the torches, we finally saw some people and I challenged them. In reply, there was no answer other than laughter. I freaked and shouted, 'Come down and try and steal our equipment and we will batter you!' The laughter got higher and longer. I then shouted, 'Come down here, you gypsy barstewards, and I will show you what fight is!' I called a 'stand to': everyone up and out of slugs (sleeping bags). The laughter was now hilarity and down walked the training staff, almost pissing themselves. I felt a right stupid twat, getting set up like that, but hey, I was fifteen and was learning all the time!

At end of the week, my group of six got a lift back; everyone else tabbed it. It was summer term, so we also had a bridging camp to look forward to, for two weeks, at Halton Camp near Lancaster. Till then, I had to go back to Charlie Chase and do all that blinking theory again. Remember, we were never going to hit it off, but at least that term, I passed. Education days were more fun though, and I was finally getting the opportunity to attain my expectations. However, one incident will never leave my mind; we were in mathematics class after our NAAFI break, tea/coffee, and cake. We were in class less than five minutes when somebody farted, and the teacher, who was a big strapping former Welsh rugby player, forgot his name, and said, 'Who did that?' A hand went up, and I say this verbatim what he said, as I have never ever forgotten it: 'Can't you control your muscles, boy?' The class burst out laughing, but me, I was nearly rolling on the floor in fits. He warned us to shut up, but no matter how hard I tried, I could not stop laughing; it cost me two days ROPs. Still, it was good. I could still have a bit of humour on me; just wait till I start underage drinking in the next chapter!

One of the most amazing events I saw at Chepstow was when the college invited the Royal Corps of Ghurkha Display Team to spend a long weekend with us. We were enthralled with these small rock-hard men, who seemed to have permanent smiles when not on duty. They gave us an amazing drill display at an amazing 180 steps per minute; read again, 180 steps per minute inch-perfect drills. During one battle, they covered 160 kilometres in eleven hours, almost unbelievable. We then went swimming and used all the camp facilities with our guests. I am so glad I remembered that snippet of information. They, of course, imbibed with the senior group and joined in at the disco. I have never in my life met strangers I would personally feel so proud of. Yet after all this, they are still treated abysmally by whoever governs Britain.

CHAPTER 10

Chepstow, the Happy Years—Section 4

Chepstow really was the making of many, many young men. Every term, there was intense competition, which was always hotly contested. This was between A, B, and C wings of J Company. Then it moved up a gear when it was senior A, B, and C companies. Injuries in all sports were prevalent. However, nothing made you prouder than winning.

In J Company, during my second term of the first term, my new platoon sergeant was Sergeant Taff Leek of the Light Infantry, who was a great guy and not really a stickler for discipline. I reckon our platoon was causing him some grief in the sergeants' mess. Drill was rubbish, turnout worse, and we were favourites to come last in the drill and turnout discipline. We had a great apprentice corporal called Jock Henney, who was a small, tough Glaswegian who gave or asked for no quarter.

We had two big guys who we felt were throwing their weight about: Big Nigel Packer, a rugby player (what else), and Dougal Adkins, his mate. Some of us thought we would take it upon ourselves to give him some retribution (me, a bully!). We all ran into his room and jumped him on his bed, sticking the boot, in etc. Nigel was hurt but said not a thing; Dougal wasn't about. Anyway, Jock got to hear of it and ordered each one of us into the toilets individually and asked three questions:

1) Were you one of the individuals?
2) Do you want to be charged?
3) Will you accept my justice?

Many of us answered 'Yes, no, yes' to the questions and came out of the toilets unable to masturbate for a few days. It did however form an alliance within the platoon. From then on, we looked after our own, no matter what.

Back to the story: The competition high spot was not hockey, football, rugby, or swimming. It was the drill and turn-out competition and 'best rooms' that decided who were 'the Cocks of the Walk'. We were outright favourites, apparently by the whole college, to come . . . *last!*

We heard this information second-hand, from the C Wing. Sergeant Farrar also taught everyone first aid and his methodology will go with me to the grave (more later). Taff had us on the square quite often, but 'Jock Henney's' bonding exercise had worked a treat: We had pride in most of our mates and were pleased to now be working as a *team*. Three or four days before the Saturday Morning Drill and Turn-out Competition, our drill was looking good, our turn-out in work clothes was still 'shite', but our No. 2 best dress was looking really good. Our brasses were looking even better than my mate Frank Hall's guardroom bell. We worked together to help each other bond. We had two guys, both called Jones, in the platoon. One was Welsh and a bit of a bully, called Blodwyn or Blod for short. The other was Jones 643, a really nice guy from somewhere in Lowestoft. Our best dress shirts were collarless and the collars were starched by us and then studded on to the shirt. Drill and Turn-out: everyone was looking and feeling great (I actually felt as nervous as I was before a big bout, so was having an adrenaline high), and we were ready.

Just a few minutes before we were due to form up, be marched to the square, be inspected by a guest of honour, then go through our drill routine, Jones 643 noticed on his final check that his collar had a small wrinkle in it. So he said, 'I will be there in a minute.' Meanwhile, we went downstairs and formed up. A minute later, Jones 643 came down obviously in agony. Instead of slipping the collar off, giving it a quick squirt of starch and iron it and then reattach it, a two-minute job, he took the red-hot iron to his collar and had an angry four-inch blister on his neck. Taff Leek immediately dismissed him and sent him to the medical room, where he was then sent on to the hospital; our friend then had a new name—'Gimpy'!

We were one short for Drill and Turn-out, and we could see Sergeant Farrer 'smirking' from the corner of our eyes. We, though, concentrated and swaggered on to the square, led by Jock Henney and controlled by Taff Leek. That day, everyone could feel the inner pride that our platoon had. We worked together, drilled excellently, and knew within ourselves that we were bloody good! When the results were read out, B Wing were the surprise winners. Not to us though; we just knew.

Sunday was always Church Parade, and many of us despised being made to go to church, so Frank Hall, I, and a few others decided it was enough. The Catholics, because we were fewer in number, were allowed to march round to church with an A/T (apprentice tradesman) marching them round the corner. I am not sure why we had so many Catholics that day, as we had planned to body swerve the church. Someone opened a ground floor window, and the Catholics, marching to church unaccompanied, as soon as we were out of the line of sight of J Company, all made a run for the open window and back into B Wing. We made our way to the top floor and, one by one, used our improving 'assault course' techniques to get in to the loft, then covered the hole with the hatch cover. This was brilliant; I had never seen so many 'Catholics' in one place, and it really was an adventure. We were speaking low and joking. Then our Gimpy, who was not a Catholic and was learning to be a plumber, stood on the copper joint to the huge water tank, which had to be at least 1000-gallon capacity. Yes, you guessed what comes next. The tank burst and 1000 gallons of water took the ceiling completely off B Wing's foyer. We got out of that building faster than we had moved in our lives.

By heavens, looking back, it was hilarious and watching the Catholics coming back into the building after our ceiling adventure, looking like angels, would have won us Oscars. No blame was attached to anyone, and emergency plumbers and plasterers were called.

To complete J Company's adventures in the second term, we had two things to look forward to: a wing talent competition and an introduction to first-aid by the aforementioned Sergeant Farrar, whom I will start with. We went to the cinema/assembly hall, and the good sergeant was there doing the spiel of pulse, heart assembly, and parts of the body, heart, lungs, etc. and CPR and emergency assistance to people bleeding to death after an accident on his skeleton borrowed from MRS. I was glad he was doing this, and not Daktari, because there were no withers or fetlocks on this skeleton! Anyway, Sgt Farrer then started asking questions and getting answers that he liked and then asked a final question: What do you do if you see someone bleeding to death in the street? We were suggesting taking our jumpers off and using that as a tourniquet, which he liked, then gave us the best solution I have ever heard. 'It is a "bloody emergency"!' he screamed for impetus. 'You grab the first woman who passes, take her bag off her, and search for sanitary towels (Tampax were rare then). Even better,' he said, 'grab an old lady who will have incontinence pads, cause they dribble in their sixties (oops, not long for me!) and use these to apply pressure to the wound until the Emergency Services get there!

The day of the talent contest came, and no one who was there will ever forget it. Each wing did their thing, and then the permanent staff had to do one as well. The top of the charts a few months earlier had been 'Grandad' by Clive Dunn and was in the charts for twenty-one weeks. So unbeknownst to us, a lot of 'pads brats' (permanent staff children) came on starting to sing the song and Sapper (soon to be lance corporal) Yates came on dragging an old bath chair as the children were completing their song, and a lot of permanent staff were fussing round this bath chair and praising and acting like grandchildren. The bath chair was turned to the audience, and there before us was CSM Phil Langley made up to look twenty-five years older than he was. At the last chorus, we, the apprentices, all sang 'Grandad, Grandad, we love you', as if we expected to see the CSM cry. He knew, though, that we really did love him. We were in hysterics; it was just absolutely audacious, and I still have those vivid memories even now! The next night, we were due to go out on our first ever platoon underage 'piss-up' as we were leaving J Company with all the scary stories of how bad it was in B Company (a bit like moving from primary to secondary school). We went down to a nice pub somewhere near Caldicot Ranges for a night out. They knew we were mostly underage, but the owner was an ex-Beachley boy, so he just 'got it'. We were having a great laugh until the nasty bugger, Blod Jones, emptied an ashtray into my final pint, thinking it hilarious that I was boking everywhere I went. So no, bullying was not quite over. I would get some more in B Company, then weeks of hell at Cove before I became a PTI and got a little bit of revenge here and there!

It was Christmas 1971 and as usual, off we would go. My uncle Frank had joined up, completed his sprog training and joined Fourth Royal Tank Regiment. He was living right across the road from the NAAFI with his family and, unknown to me, my wee brother Tam. I got to Franks prior to going to Dundee as a group only to find Frank furious. My young brother only took the opportunity to burgle the NAAFI, going back three times and filling the equivalent of a wheelie bin with spirits. Alas, he must have been Irish in another life, because in the heavy snow was a blood pathway all the way to Frank's as any military policeman, indeed even Mr McGoo, could follow the trail. Frank said Tam was in Wakefield Prison, as he was not getting bail and there was no room in any young offenders' facility.

I reckon that is where his sexual preferences changed; seems ridiculous to put a fifteen-year-old in a top security prison. Anyway, I said I would go and get a drink to cheer him up and brought back a bottle of dark rum, only to notice it had a red blood thumb mark on it. Here was me buying what I could have drank for nothing if Tam had an ounce of sense and stem the blood or went and brushed away his path of blood.

CHAPTER 11

Chepstow, the Happy Years—Section 5

I am going to use this chapter to round up the Chepstow years, some of our great tricks, and of course my British title. We went to Halton Bridging Camp in Lancaster in June 1971 to learn the 'must knows' of a sapper: Learn to build bridges across the River Lune, camp under canvas, and to use our spare time wisely, normally looking for a girl. It was a great experience going up the M6 in old army coaches to learn new things that we find funny now. Bailey Bridges* came palletised then, with lifting bars to lift the sections. Remember, no health and safety or risk assessments in the 1970s. A bridge panel was bloody heavy, weighing in at 570 lbs but was deemed a six-man lift even though the men were only wee boys.

*The *Bailey bridge* is a type of portable, pre-fabricated, truss bridge. It was developed by the British during World War II for military use and saw extensive use by both British and American military engineering units.

A Bailey bridge had the advantages of requiring no special tools or heavy equipment to construct. The wood and steel bridge elements were small and light enough to be carried in trucks and lifted into place by hand, without requiring the use of a crane. The bridges were strong enough to carry tanks. Bailey bridges continue to be extensively used in civil engineering construction projects and to provide temporary crossings for foot and vehicle traffic. It was a really simple design like a big jigsaw with two large steel pins holding it together. The 'pin man' had to be brave and fast, as in operation, many people lost fingers ramming the pin home. We also built easier bridges and learnt river craft, all good fun. I got my first girlfriend attracted by the uniform, and we, like many apprentices, spent time at the canal or the Williamson Memorial in the park and one day in Morecambe.

Like 99 per cent of victims, I wear my heart on my sleeve, thinking any sign of affection was love. Anyway, we went back to Chepstow at the end of the fortnight, and I was writing ballads every second day and getting answers. She asked me to come up mid-term and I was delighted, only to find nobody to meet me at Lancaster Station. I went to her house and there she was, all comfy with a new boyfriend!

Really embarrassed and hurt, I headed back to Chepstow and arrived Saturday morning, seventy-two hours too early. I went to my room and got changed into my sweat equipment, went up to the old gym, and worked out until I collapsed. The feeling of exhaustion had overcome me, but with it came a massive endorphin kick; it was then I knew I did not want to be an electrician; I wanted this exhilaration on a regular basis.

Got another telling off for coming back early, but it was no big deal, as my bed was there and I had a daily duty cook! I continued my trade training and at the mid-point of Term 5 (which was six for me), I had achieved an A3 electrician grade but was informed alongside my good mate Eddie Harwood RIP (the only man I ever charged in the Army) that we would not be sitting our city and guilds exam; instead, we were given jobs like putting in electric heaters. Now I was out of camp more than most others anyway, boxing almost fortnightly against the Open-Class Senior boxers in Wales and south-west England and learning many things. Every weekend from the first term, I was away playing hockey, and remember Sergeant Cox who initially met us at Chepstow? Well, I had a real blow out with him refereeing our company hockey match against C Company and was sent off for calling him useless; he attempted to charge me but couldn't, as rank disappeared on sports fields for obvious reasons.

By that time, a lot of us had a dilemma. We liked to go to Bristol on Friday nights; however, due to bus timings, there was no way to get back before 23.59; yet, being an adult now, I now know that had we gone and explained it to our CSM, we would have got the extra hour without too much of a problem. Anyway, Frank Hall, usually our ringleader, and four or five of us came up with a plan. We would get the 22.15 bus from Bristol after chasing girls, and then we would get off the bus at the Chepstow end of the Severn Bridge, run back across the bridge to where the painters' gantries were. We would then come down the gantry and drop the twenty or thirty feet into camp, depending on where the gantry was; we were paratroopers before our time. Now remember the camp was guarded, so we would then run down to the point and come along the River Wye shoreline, till we got near our playing fields, then run up past the workshops, and up to the guardroom at roughly 23.49, ten minutes inside the allotted time. Yes, as Steve Harley sang: 'Those were the best years of our life.' Truly!

I had a real problem in fourth term (fifth for me), around the same time as the Army Championship Boxing at Chepstow—an opportunity to pose! It was the day of the finals; I was due in Oswestry once more for the Western District Hockey Championships. Captain Smith said I had to play hockey, me: I was boxing—ENDEX. At 7 p.m. on the Thursday evening, I was in the ring and boxing well within myself, winning easily. I checked the draw and was due to box again at 2 p.m. the following day, so I went to the cookhouse and duty cook made me a largish meal. I went back to my room and Captain Smith came walking in. I stood to attention expecting a bollocking, as he said, 'I have managed to bring your semi-final forward to 9.20 tonight.'

I was in shock: stomach full! Nevertheless, I went to the gym, got dressed again, and lay on the high board of the swimming pool trying to relax. My name was called, I went and got gloved up, and climbed into the ring. It was a cracking fight against someone called Eden-Winn of Arborfield Apprentice College. I thought I had done more than enough to win. The judges were taking an eternity coming to a decision, and in fact, they all got together to argue the decision, I knew something funny was happening; I lost my first military boxing match 3-2 and was livid. Captain Smith had somehow got his way. So it was Oswestry next morning for the hockey, which we won again, even more convincingly. Being petulant, I deliberately missed a kick out of the D, giving the infantry an early lead. I did not have anything else to deal with, as Tony Hines, Tony Winn, and Wally Wallace, all brilliant players, took the other side apart. We won 9-1. You can take it from me, though, Capt Smith knew I was not a good loser!

In Term 6, I had qualified for the semi-finals of the National Association of Boys Clubs by knocking out a young man from Sandy in Bedfordshire at The Aston Manor Boys Club in Birmingham. Then mayhem ensued, as Daktari got to hear about it and I was ordered to the medical room, where he deemed me too thin and put me on a protein and yeast extract diet to ensure I was too heavy for the fight. I explained the situation to one of the friendly medics (there were a few) and he recorded that I had taken the yeast extract (well the sink did) and was now four pounds heavier. Daktari released me; I went and checked my weight. I was a pound over and our B Company sergeant, Dave McFarlane, took me through to Newport. There, I had a sauna and massage and became underweight when I received a letter through the mail telling me I had a bye to the final, as the person I was boxing could not make the grade. Oddly, no one came and checked my weight, neither did I have to go and weigh in and walkover, as was usual.

I had already decided I was moving into the senior group and passing out of Chepstow. To me, there was no point in staying at Chepstow, though I loved it, only to do odd jobs with Eddie for another term. I applied to our CSM, a huge Scots Guardsman, and it was approved. But I would have to join two days late, as my NABC final was scheduled for 16 March 1973 in St Patrick's Social Club in Leeds. I had then heard the whole of my platoon were coming to support me, and I wanted to let no one down. I was dead on weight; I travelled up in the morning with a captain who was in charge of boxing at the time and Charlie Booth, the coach of Underwood ABC, whose badge I was boxing under. Luckily, they boxed in black or I would have worn my Chepstow vest. I remember hanging around from lunchtime starving and then being taken to a cinema to relax; it didn't work. I couldn't sit for more than five minutes, as Adrenaline was coursing through my body. I told the captain to enjoy the film and that I would meet him outside in ninety minutes and just went for a stroll.

When we eventually got to the social club, it was buzzing, and 71B were at the bar singing. I then remember being terrified to climb the stairs for the weigh-in and my body felt like it weighed a ton. I got there eventually, and the room was full of very talented boxers, including George Feeney, Ricky Beaumont, and Clinton McKenzie, who all went on to great things in the pro ranks. I jumped on the scales and was 8st 6lbs, one pound underweight. The clerk of the scales agreed, and my opponent's trainer went berserk, demanding I go back on the scales. I told him to go f*ck himself. The reason soon became clear: David Coombes, my opponent, was one pound over and therefore had to sweat it off.

I will never ever forget the reception I got when I stepped into the ring; every hair on my body was standing on end; I had hair everywhere; I was buzzing. We were brought to the centre of the ring and David tried to do the stare. I smiled brightly and looked down; he thought he was winning. This to me, though, was going to be my proof to the lads that I was no failure. My favourite shot as a southpaw was to parry his left lead, step in, and hook to the solar plexus. I was ahead and at the start of last round, David charged out of his corner straight on to my parry, and I released an uppercut. Down he went like the Berlin wall; I was so hyped I ran to the neutral corner and was shouting, 'Get up! C'mon, get up!' He did not and I was NABC champion. I was pipped for boxer of the night by Clinton McKenzie, certainly no disgrace. So there was I, the wee tinker from Dundee, achieving what I had promised when I was attacked by the paedophile! Travelling back with the old platoon was brilliant; I had made them feel good and they me.

The next morning, I was driven to Cribbs Causeway Camp near Bristol (now a huge shopping complex) to join up with the senior group. Waiting for me was Sergeant Bill Cummings of A Company, who had little time for me and gave me a real beasting, saying to me, 'You might be a champion, but to me, you are fuck all' and 'If fancied a go, then just ask!' He issued me a large heavy shell and made me run three times round the large triangle with it above my head. Nevertheless, I coped with everything thrown at me, and more. We were forced to scrub our spider and had kit inspections and weapon drills almost constantly. This was to prove very useful to get ready for Cove.

Anyway, before pass-out was the prize-giving, I participated in hockey, athletics, cross country running, and boxed for the college and had my triple-coloured lanyard for three sports since Term 4. However, there was no doubt in my mind, and in many others, the best all-round sportsman was not me, but Tony Hines, who was a wizard and excellent at every sport he did, alongside being an excellent soldier. I got the Best Sportsman trophy and the Cyril Gailee Boxing Trophy for the third time; never happened before or since. I went to Tony and apologised. Tony, being the man he was, was magnanimous and told me I deserved it for the boxing alone.

The next morning, we lined up and got ready to pass out; we marched on to the square again with a swagger. At the end of the parade, all the other apprentices formed a space which 'Senior Group' marched through to pass out. I couldn't believe we were spat on by some of the younger ones; I had never expected that. Apparently, though, it had been going on for years, though I had no memories of it. Our military equipment was then transported to Cove by a four-tonner, ready for us to begin getting shit all over again. We meanwhile went on two weeks leave, preparing for the dramas ahead. Goodbye, Chepstow. You gave me my lifetime's fondest memories.

Just over a month ago, I was sent a message on Facebook which made me so proud it made me weep. I think as I leave Chepstow behind, it is time to thank Sergeant Ivan Edwards, known to us apprentices as Muskie, by adding this tearjerker. Ivan, you have really no idea what this meant and especially at the time I got it!

'I remember a smart, quiet, young Apprentice L/Cpl as tough as a Rhino with the courage of a Lion but with a pure heart and as gentle as a lamb inside. The best boxer ever to pass through the gates at Beachley. Bet you can't remember me?'

CHAPTER 12

Cove, the Learning Curve

In April 1973, we arrived at Cove individually knowing it wouldn't be any worse than our pre-training at Cribbs Causeway. We had been warned to look out for 'strange individuals'. We expected 'gays' (I despise the way the word, which meant happy then, has been stolen), although it was not allowed at that time. We arrived in dribs and drabs and collected our Chepstow kit from a storeroom. Settling in and given a bit of leeway in comparison to new recruits, in walked this 'strange individual': I was not going near, as I was obviously afraid of gays, who for some reason I thought were paedophiles, due to the issues I had. I no longer object to homosexuals, but I do object to them using the word 'gay', which to me infers they are happier than us. Anyway, he had a group around him and he was showing a book and reading a script; turns out he was selling insurance as a side line! In walked our troop corporal (the other corporal scurried out without even a word). Corporal Hughes, another Scot, did not like me; it was plain from the look on his ugly face. Despite us all being semi-trained and prepared, I was not ready to be sent to see the world's worst barber. He was lopsided, and as you went to the chair, his first question was 'Something for the weekend?' If your answer was no, you got a screamer of a scalped haircut, making you look like a US Marine. If it was yes, you bought his condoms and got a reasonable cut. Oh well, I learnt another lesson I would never forget.

After our haircut, we were sent to the slophouse for food. I honestly think the Army Catering Corps sent their worst cooks there; the food was vile. We needed to eat though, as building strength was important for the training ahead. We were still scum in the minds of the training staff and were beasted quite often, but hey, our wages had increased, as we had left

Boy Service behind, and after these twelve weeks, we would be on our way to new postings anywhere in the world. We were joined by the guys from Rhyl and Dover Junior Leaders, mostly good guys, but as usual, a bully was present and tried to make himself the boss. Corporal Hughes made him Room I/C. I am not naming him or others, mainly because I cannot remember them; however, I seemed to have the worst room jobs, not that I gave a monkey's; I had become a national champion only eight weeks earlier and it had just sunk in.

I got a letter the next day inviting me to box for Young Scotland against Young England in four weeks time in Guildford. I had a bit of sense, realising I could not do it justice, whilst in the middle of so much 'sapper work'. I called Frank Henry and explained; he was fine about it and told me I would have had a great fight with George Feeney, who I had met at the finals. When I got the letter, I told Hughes. He said, 'Please get me a ticket. I would love to go.' I told him I had turned the opportunity down due to the training. I was called a bloody fool, but I knew what was required; he did not!

The SSM of Fifty-seven Squadron was a nasty 'bar steward' and found fault with the efforts of ex-boy soldiers for the stupidest of things in order to shout, scream, and attempt to break them. He really must have left every night with a screaming headache. When he went off on one, you could see the veins and arteries clearly in his head: not a good sign. We were given the rules of conduct: We would run absolutely everywhere on camp. We would come to attention every time a lance corporal or upwards spoke to us. We would be required to do one guard duty every two weeks and one fire picket a month. During training, we would not talk except whilst on NAAFI breaks or when we were asked questions. Then we were shown round the whole camp at running pace, but really, that was no big deal after Cribbs, and we knew we would be fine. The training staff, we quickly learnt, were firm, fair, and usually friendly, but infringe the rules and you were going to be charged and lose money.

I loved the training: using mine detectors, then prodding for and disarming the mines, building all types of constructions, and doing night exercises around Hawley Lake. I do not remember ever getting much PT while we were there; it was more hands-on soldiering. I will never forget that after about six weeks and just before our first long weekend, we had a camp lockdown. We were told that there would be explosives brought into camp and it was our job to stop this from occurring. We were put in charge of the guardroom area and would monitor everyone coming into camp, including the cars. This was fun but with real dangers being put into our head.

There seemed to me to be an awful lot of staff coming into camp in cars, and as we were searching the cars, the others behind would show impatience and beep horns; those on foot would just try to walk past. Regardless of who they were, we stopped them. We had found quite a lot of stuff just in the morning, but at lunchtime, this one corporal, who had driven out at 10.00 hours, drove back in with a plaster cast on his arm. To me, it looked wrong, as there was no hand support on it and it started at the wrist. I questioned him as to why his cast had no hand support. He gave a plausible answer; it was to allow him to drive, as he was going on leave. However, I was still not happy and went to grab the plaster; he screamed as if in agony. I then agreed and let him through. At the end of the exercise, the troop was shown the amount of dangerous equipment we had allowed in. The training staff were impressed at the amount we had stopped. The corporal I had queried stood up, his plaster now off, and showed his contraband of fifty rounds of 7.62 mm ammunition. He actually praised me and said I showed initiative, but no balls! He said to me to always go with your first instinct, regardless of the circumstances: another valuable lesson learnt.

We were now at the halfway stage, with a weekend off for most of the camp. I remember going to Aldershot on the piss and grabbing a lady. After taking her home, I had missed the bus, so I stupidly thumbed a lift up Queens Avenue and got a lift from, yes, another gay man. He was made to regret trying it on. Three hundred metres from camp, he pulled into the side and said, 'Well, son, it is payback time.'

I thought, 'Oh fuck! Why me again?' This time I had had more than enough. I immediately pulled him towards me and head-butted him. I got out of the car, went around to the driver's side, and pulled him out of the car. I kneed him in the crotch and hooked him in the solar plexus, then strolled away not even looking back. Yes, stronger but still naïve. I got back to my room and a voice asked me to leave the lights off; I did and just got into bed. Within a matter of minutes, I could hear moaning and asked Keith if he was all right. I thought he was having a nightmare. Another guy in the room, who also did not go on leave, said, 'He will be OK. Don't worry.' The moaning (in different tones) went on for such a long time, but I had then drifted off to sleep. In the morning, I was woken by noises of people going out. There, at the bottom of my bed were the two guys, both with a woman each. I felt a right stupid prat!

I had been going to the gym at night and applied to become an assistant physical training instructor. I had to pass five tests before I could be accepted on the course, four of which I passed within five minutes, but try as I might,

I could not do a handspring. Whilst being taught how, I ran up to do one and the light mat slipped, tearing every ligament in my right ankle. The SSM PT said, 'I will pass you and will see you in six weeks after training. You will go on the PTI course in September.' I was really chuffed but had to hobble everywhere for a week or so.

The final memory of training was going to Salisbury Plain. Each group had to blow up a long rectangular boxed girder into two pieces. The training corporals gave us a formula, and once we had worked out how much plastic explosive we required, we had to raise our hand and one of the training staff would issue us our requested amount of plastic explosive. Corporal Hughes just said, 'You might get a wee crack if that is all you want!' I was a little perturbed, as this stuff was already sweating, not the best of signs. Anyway, I had worked out that so long as we packed the explosive at the same point on all four sides of the girder, it would work. We worked for five minutes, packing it into four L-shaped gaps, then secured the PE with four flat bits of wood and tied wood round each portion of sweaty PE. We then used four detonators instead of two, and you don't want to know where I got the extras from. Anyway, we inserted detonators and connected the detonation cord to this sweaty Fred Carno's Army attempt. I got one of my partners to distract Corporal Hughes while I connected the four detonators to the detonation box. Then, when permission was given, you would wind the handle furiously to build up a current and press the button. The girder could not have been cut better if we had used a hacksaw. There was a huge cheeky smile from me! One group had to make a second attempt, as they had lost their detonators in the gorse.

One final story from the days in Fifty-seven Squadron: One of the guys had this girl. He met her after getting tickets for Top of the Pops; he used to hide her in our drying room, and we kept things quiet, until items of equipment and small amounts of money started going missing. Corporal Hughes was going to get in the Military Police to sort it out; the culprit, however, admitted it was him. It was the guy whose girl we were shielding. Anyway, he got a kicking from us and was marched to the guardroom, charged, jailed for twenty-eight days, and discharged. We saw this as a great opportunity to get back a kit we had lost (not had stolen), as it would save us money. So a list asking us to declare items that had been stolen from us went around; when it came back, you could have fully kitted out half a troop! Give the guy his due, he pleaded guilty to everything, and we were all reissued with our lost kit, giving us a full kit before our final checks at Cove. Sapper initiative or theft, make your own mind up. The next day, our postings were put up on the board. I was due to go to Thirty-eight Engineer Regiment at Waterbeach near Cambridge (apparently a good posting for a first one), but I already knew I was going to First Training Regiment as a local-acting lance corporal. The time to move out came; we all shook hands and made our way to squadrons around the world. Me, I just walked across camp into the world of First Training Regiment Royal Engineers to prepare for my September PTI course.

CHAPTER 13

First Training Regiment and Corporals' Mess

On 3 September 1973, I tacked on my local-acting lance corporal's stripe and was issued with a room key. I went into the room not knowing what to expect, as there was no one at home. Two hours later, my roommate, Cpl John Moorhouse from Ninth Squadron RE and on attachment looked me up and down. I could imagine exactly what he was thinking: 'sprog' and 'craphat' being but two of his thoughts. John was a soft-spoken Irishman and was very laid back; he invited me to go to the corporals' mess with him. I was eighteen years and four days old and very unsure of myself, so I refused and just generally tidied up my gear and tried on my itchy Dennis the Menace jumper. Yup, it felt good, but exactly what was I letting myself in for? Well I got my very first 'shower' about 3 a.m. John had come in rat-arsed and went straight to bed; like a lot of engineers, he had lost his bearings whilst drunk and pissed all over me and my bed. I screamed like a banshee, never imagining this. It woke John from his pissing slumber; he stopped and went to the toilet to dump the last little bit of my shower. He came back in the room and said, 'Serves you right for being a craphat. I will fix it in the morning!' I slept no longer that night and turned up early at the gym after showering and shaving. On getting back that evening, John was as good as his word; my bed had been taken away and he had got me a new mattress, sheets, and blankets and had even made it up for me French-style with loads of frills at the bottom . . . ouch!

Anyway, on arriving at the gym, I was told by the SSM (I forget his name) that he had a treat for me; I was to first go meet Staff Sergeant Joe Keirnan and then run for First Training Regiment in a cross-country event at Tweezledown Racecourse and the tank tracks, which I would soon know extremely intimately! I put on my Scotland tracksuit for the kudos; I had to at least feel the part. I turned up at the gym. Staff Sergeant Keirnan was teaching an Amateur Boxing Association Coaching Course. Joe welcomed me and said, 'What can you do?' I had no idea what he was on about, so he asked me to glove up. In the other corner was Paul Mehrlich, the current Army Senior Champion. We sparred for three rounds; now, I had not really trained in three months and had my birthday in Dundee just a few days before (no excuses), but I more than comfortably held my own. I was then introduced to the current ABA champion at bantamweight, Norman Phillips, with whom I sparred a few rounds and who showed me my shortcomings. However, I was asked to join the Army team immediately. I explained that I was going to do my APTI course, which finished at the end of October. Joe said, 'Meet me at Maida Gym after the course. Meanwhile, come up on sparring nights, Tuesdays, and see how you do!'

I was chuffed and then had to go run a ten-kilometre tough cross-country race. It began at 14.00 over a very wet, muddy racecourse and even muddier tank tracks. I ran fairly well and came in twenty-second, but I was disappointed, as I hate losing. However, it turned out I was first in the Under-21 Category, so had inadvertently become a cross-country champion. Not bad at all for my first full day as a trained sapper and APTI.

The SSM was proud but reiterated that unless I got a merit on my PTI Course, I would not be kept at Cove and could go to any unit at twenty-four hours' notice. Honestly, apart from handsprings, the course to me was an absolute doddle; I expected a merit. However, as usual, I undid all my good work by putting my big mouth into gear. We were out running with a coloured, newly promoted sergeant and my platoon leader whilst on course, Andy Crouch, a great guy, and I believe he was an ex-para. He said, 'OK, lads, a long slog of cross country today. I want to introduce you to the tank tracks. This will show the men from the boys.' We jogged from Fox Lines all the way to tank tracks, passing the QARANC Unit (Queen Alexandria Royal Army Nursing Corps)—*women* for future memory. Not for me, though I still had real self-confidence issues and had no idea why. I was bright and cheerful when I went out with the boxing team lads and was, I thought, funny and chatty, but me and 'Pamela Right' always seemed to go home alone.

We turned the corner and had to do a few hill runs to warm us up after the three miles we had already run and then prepared for the tank tracks; these were very deep, very muddy, and very wet due to unseasonal weather. Andy said, 'Right, guys, this is your endurance test. Do not worry about time, though you will fail if seen walking!' He set off at quite a clip over the mud, and I was ten metres behind him but unusually, extremely comfortable. I then decided to make a race of it, and within two minutes, I had drawn alongside Andy and then just got my chest in front and turned to smile. Andy said, 'Stay in line with me!'

Gobby here said, 'Why? Can't you do the pace?' and moved ahead.

Andy caught up and said, 'You are one gobby little shite, and no matter how good you are, I am marking you down.'

At that, I stepped up my pace and beat Andy by roughly fifteen metres. He was livid. Unbeknownst to me, there was a bus back to Fox Lines. Not for me, though. I was made to about-turn and go back the way I came. When, oh when, would I learn to keep my big gob shut?

As it was an autumn course, it was the worst course, because every day, we had the duty of keeping Queens Avenue completely leaf-free. We used to go out at 07.00, after breakfast at Hammersley Barracks and then walk down the avenue with huge bin bags picking up the leaves. Andy Crouch, my platoon boss, decided we required another long run, just to teach us a wee lesson. It really was incredible; we ran to Church Crookham, about seven miles away; it was then the barracks of the Ghurka Regiment. The first thing we thought—they must have had colder weather than us? It could not be possible that we had only run seven miles, as there was not one single leaf dying on the trees and the camp was immaculate. Andy made us mark time and turn inward to face the camp.

We noted there was a soldier up the tree shaking it till the leaves dropped. Andy said, 'There is efficiency for you, lads,' and turned us round to run the seven miles back to Hammersley; fourteen bloody miles to see a Ghurkha shake a tree!

Andy was true to his word as far as aptitudes. I got a pass with the following remarks: 'A great student with many fantastic qualities. However, requires maturity and must learn to keep his mouth shut before attending the Advanced Course.'

I got back to Cove knowing I could go any day and was working as hard as possible in all I could do, even perfecting handsprings. I enjoyed the camaraderie of the corporals' mess at the training regiment, as I had qualified through hard work and deserved my tape. You have to remember, a lot of the training NCOs really had no time to associate, and very few that I asked if they actually enjoyed being training NCOs, their answers were almost the same, 'There are only so many beastings you can give before it gets boring.' Then the job just becomes a chore, with working all day and room inspections at night. They told me the first three weeks were the worst; then they got to know the characters in their platoons, who they would give status to knowing the unseen work was being completed. To them, the only good thing was training NCOs got on senior NCOs cadres quicker, so long as they had left their mark. There were also a lot of unaware recruits who were being taught milling in the gym, when suddenly, one of the senior staff would ask the recruits if they fancied milling with Lance Corporal Curran, the smallest APTI in Cove. Quite a few hands went up in every class, an opportunity to thump an NCO for free! So they would set up four benches and it would start off nice; then the recruit usually lost his temper. That was always the point I threw two hooks to the lower ribs, and the recruit would be on the floor gasping but asking how he got there. Once, I was caught out bonnie though; the questions were being asked as per usual and this group was very cute. They opened up a funnel. At the back was this coloured guy who said, 'I wouldn't mind a go, Corporal.'

I didn't really know fear, but even I was seriously worried when I saw this recruit's body and muscle tone. He must have had three stone on me; I just wanted out and immediately threw the left-right hooks to the floating rib and this guy just did not flinch. To help you understand, that is like booting someone right in the balls and he smiles at you. He was strong and tough; every time he hit me, it hurt, so much so that I had to cheat to get out of there! I ensured he came forward throwing his punches; that was until my ankles felt the wood of the bench. I then backward-dived Suarez-style and made out I had tripped and hurt the back of my head.

I had a few drinks with Corporal Hughes and John Moorhouse; the booze flowed and was considerably cheaper than the NAAFI, but generally, I was getting ready to join the Army boxing team, which was my next plan. On 1 November, my posting came to Eighteenth Squadron—12 RSME. I had to be there the following day. So I rushed, getting all my kit together, and was allowed to leave my sports equipment at Maida Gym, home of the Army boxing team.

I arrived at Strood Railway Station, and transport took me out to Chattenden Barracks, where I was given my own room (Wow!) and my own personal keys to the gymnasium, which would come in handy on disco nights. I then met RSM Paddy Haslett, who explained my job in these terms: 'Go to the Army boxing team until end of season (March/April). Then come back, get the plant operator mechanics fit (yeah, right), and run our potential officer course in May. Help wherever you are required, and it will all go well.' The definition of insane in the Royal Engineers was someone trying to get a plant operator mechanic fit; they sat on their backsides all day with plenty of snacks hidden. So I just worried about the Battle Fitness Test, which was a doddle even for pensioners!

So there I was, 2 November 1973, just over eighteen and seconded to the Army boxing team until April, unless I was eliminated from the national championships.

Returning from Strood Railway Station to Aldershot quick smart, very excited, yet with obvious misgivings as I would be the young learner, and Joe never allowed his team to go pit-a-pat. He was strict and there were fines for a lot of things, in particular smoking. Brian Cherry, my sapper buddy, smoked like a chimney and always got caught. Fines actually went towards our end-of-season piss-up. I did not pay much; I despised sparring and saw no point in being hit for nothing, so used to skive and got fined for that.

CHAPTER 14

The Chattenden Years

I then left for Aldershot and was the youngest member of the team, still naive but learning extremely quickly; not as quick as I should have, though. Jimmy Matthews said, 'Welcome, Bob, have a piece of chocolate. So I broke off a fair-sized chunk of plain chocolate. I had never heard of Ex Lax before, but less than an hour later, I knew exactly what it was for. I must have spent two hours in the toilet; my backside was red raw wiping every few minutes . . . funny not!

I eventually joined the Army boxing team as a youngster and not very sure what to expect. I met some great guys, who were all ABA champions and England Internationals, Jim Matthews, Royal Green Jackets, Roger Maxwell, and Norman Phillips. I was welcomed and felt part of the team before ever getting into the ring. We trained extremely hard, always encouraging each other to get the best out of it.

Joe Keirnan, RIP, was possibly the best coach I ever worked under. He wanted things done I would never dream of attempting. The day would always start at 8 a.m. with a three-mile run to the tank tracks and special hill I have told you about; only difference was we worked for at least twenty minutes on the hill, even going backwards. The real thing was that although we bonded well as a team, we also were all extremely competitive and wanted to be winners.

On Friday, 23 November, Joe approached me and Chris Foy and asked if we fancied boxing Chris Davies at featherweight against Wales the following Friday in Stoke-on-Trent.

I said, 'Joe, I beat him in LLandaff last year!' I therefore selected myself. We arrived at Victoria Hotel in Hanley for our two-day stay, ate like a horse, had never actually been in a hotel in my life, did a bit of light training on the Friday morning, and as the Welsh team were arriving at night, the weigh-in was scheduled for 1800 hours. I went to the weigh-in and I made nine stone, and they called for Chris; he came forward. I had never seen this Chris Davies in my life and told Joe. In all my time on the Army team, I fought a lot of fantastic boxers, winning a lot of bouts but I took two hidings.

You guessed it; this Chris Davies came out of the corner and stopped me, after first giving me a two-minute boxing lesson. It turned out that Charlie Booth had told him all about my body shots, and Chris was not falling for them. Chris went on to become European Professional Light Welterweight Champion, so no disgrace really. After that hiding, to make matters worse, I was going to a place near Aberystwyth to get engaged to a girl I had been seeing for just a few months at PT School, heart on my sleeve, falling in 'love', and asking to marry. We were to meet at Crewe Station for the journey to her parents' place. All went well; we met up, and we went to her home, went for the ring, then a few drinks, and despite the abuse I was getting from another competitive person, 'her' I was happy with. On Sunday, we went to see the minister about the marriage and everything was settled. I still have no reason why, but three days later, I received a bad encounter with cold feet and called the whole thing off. There are times when I do still say, 'If only . . .'

Life sometimes makes you make mistakes to make you stronger, however I was making so many.

We returned and Army Intermediate Championships were taking place, and Joe really wanted to see what I was made of and arranged a bout with a very experienced Army boxer from the Royal Green Jackets, John 'Jake' Cheetham. Jimmy Matthews was from the same regiment, but the Army team was winding me up for days, telling me Jake was far too good for me and would give me a doing!

Our bout was the very last bout of the evening, as we were both Open Class. Joe, being the great coach he was, wanted to watch the bout, and Company Sergeant Major White, Physical Training Corps, was my allotted second.

I boxed probably my best bout as an Army team member, winning every round. Jake was a fantastic opponent and we still talk to this day.

Yeah, I was learning. My next bout was in the very same gym three weeks later against the RAF, and it was arranged to be recorded so we could all watch ourselves under scrutiny. I was told the score would be 9-2 to us, and I would be one of the losers. I was fighting their second best man, Billy Hutchinson, and he was a big hitter. I went in and the score was 4-0 to the Army. I was determined not to blot the copy book and 'ran' for three rounds, popping out loads of excellent counter punches and won well. Billy asked why he had never heard of me!

We ran out 11-0 winners, the first time a whitewash had occurred in inter-service boxing.

The next morning, we were excused our Hill Run to watch the video of the night before. I was watching my fight intently, and though I won well, I honestly looked like a baby giraffe; my legs looked unsteady, even without getting hit. I decided there and then that I had to change styles slightly, attacking with faster shots but slowing down my feet.

Only funny story of my time with the team was when I slept next to the other sapper in the team, who acted as a big brother to me, Brian Joseph Cherry, Fifty-nine Commando R.E. I was woken at about 01.30 by a not bad-looking woman. She asked me how to get to Guildford. I said to her, 'Go down to the traffic lights, turn right, and it's ten miles down the road.'

Her reply was, 'That is too far. Can I sleep with you?'

C'mon, eighteen and laid on a plate, I said, '*Yes, please*!'

At this, Brian, who had been listening, shouted to me, 'Bob, no, mate!'

So, listening to Brian, I reluctantly said, 'No!'

I heard her go to the next four beds, where she was welcomed with open arms. In the morning, six members of the Army boxing team had a dose of the 'clap'! Cheers, Brian.

Two weeks later, we went to Portsmouth to box the Navy. I won well and met a Wren, again fell in love, but it was stupid and I knew that in the morning. We travelled back to Aldershot and prepared for the Army championships, which was the first step in the ABA Competition. I was drawn against Steve Phillips in the semi-finals, as there were a few withdrawals, perhaps because of my performances since the Wales match? Now Steve was an assistant PTI at Chepstow and had been rather naughty, telling the other staff who knew me that he had beaten me. Steve was obviously just mistaken, as I was with Chris Davies. The bout started, I came to the ring centre and immediately hooked him deliberately low (for telling porkies). I was quietly warned by the referee; after I did it again, he would throw me out without any public warnings. Steve was good and was a worker, however, towards the end of the second round, I hooked him to the solar plexus, spot on, followed by a right hook to the chin. Steve went down and the referee called it off.

My final was against Corporal Thomson of the Parachute Regiment in the Para Gym. As I went to the ring, the booing and hissing was amazing; all these Paras and I was going to teach him a lesson. I loved boxing in adversity! Suffice to say, at the end of the bout, there was only going to be one winner, and I, in a way, single-handedly shut up the entire Second Parachute Regiment. I was now Army Senior Champion at eighteen and had a lot of dreams ahead. I still cannot believe how relaxed I looked.

Bob boxing as army champion.

Combined Services Finals were only four weeks away, and I wanted that as well. The seeding should have sorted who got the bye into the final, and as I had beaten both men in the last eight weeks, I expected it. However, Billy, as current champion, was given it, and I boxed Chats Harris of the Navy again! Calamity! He hit me with my own shot, the uppercut to the body; it hurt like hell and I was rolling on the floor. However, I shook it off and then went on to outbox him and win easily. My next title was but twenty-two hours away, so far as I was concerned. At the Nelson Gym next evening, facing my RAF adversity, I was boxing really slow, and Billy was obviously surprised I wasn't running this time but counter-punching well and after two rounds was miles ahead on points. Joe had said, 'Keep it going and keep your hands high. Billy will come out with all guns blazing and you will tire after yesterday.'

I smiled the gum shield in and out I went, feeling good; I was dealing with everything he threw at me and actually thought I had done it! Joe was correct. Billy was throwing everything and hit me with a right hook to the point of the jaw with fifteen seconds remaining; down I went, and out of the corner of my eyes, I could see Billy jumping. I was determined to get up and was up at seven, but my legs really were like that baby giraffe previously mentioned and the referee called it off despite my protest . . . Game over for that year! The very next day, I was returned to the unit until the following season; I would be stronger.

Back to Eighteen Squadron, Twelve Royal School of Mechanical Engineering. I was back for a long summer, knowing no one, but as previously mentioned, had my own room and keys to the gym, where I was in sole control unless WRAC (Women's Royal Army Corps) wanted the use of it. This is no longer the case, as women just go and select the trade and corps they would like to go to now! However, suffice to say, I loved Chattenden. Both Seventeen and Eighteen Squadron sergeant majors had knee problems and desired to build up the ligaments and joints further to surgery. I remembered our bully PT teacher at school giving our best footballer, Jimmy Kyles, some therapy to help his knee problem. I only copied it verbatim from my memory. Hey, presto! Two happy sergeant majors no longer required surgery and were great to me.

I, alongside the Chatham PTI, designed the obstacle course and initiative tests for prospective officers, part of which was to see how they would deal with tough situations. We had rigged a death slide from a large oak tree and just left it, never thinking to test it.

The next morning, the Twenty-four Potential Officers arrived. I immediately took them out on the Battle Fitness Test, then into the gym for thirty minutes of grief. They then divided into four groups of six for the initiative tests, which were not even difficult. As usual, one or two took control and got things done correctly. Finally, I took them to the Oak Tree Slide. I had grabbed six canvas toggles from the gym and demonstrated the mini-Tarzan course so they knew how to get to the top of the tree. The slide was tight and everything should have been perfect, except I had forgotten to soak the toggle. I left the platform like an action man, but ten feet down, the canvas toggle stuck due to friction. Suffice to say, I had to let go and drop twenty feet into a nettle patch. I landed correctly and made light of the error. I then asked what I did wrong. No one had any idea, so I then soaked the toggle and went round the course again; this time, everything went correctly and a catcher stopped me at the bottom successfully.

At that time, two unknown events happened to ruin my boxing career.

1) The trainer Charlie Booth from Wales went to Dundee to see my club coach Ned Lynch, who agreed, then my mum, who vehemently refused to allow me to prepare for the 1976 Olympic Games. Meanwhile, Andy Smith, the formidable manager of Dave Boy Green and Joe Bugner, had offered my RSM, Paddy Haslett, my buy-out money plus £5000 to allow me to turn professional.

Crazy money. I was only eighteen and this was 1973! I honestly thought I had made it, and like many, many footballers, I stopped progressing!

Paddy was brilliant; he sat me down like a father and explained all the implications of either decisions. I decided after a few pints of 8p Scrumpy in the NAAFI to give it another year in the amateurs, when I really did expect to win the ABA title.

Anyway, by then, I had a few senior personnel on my friends' list, and to be honest, did not have an enemy I knew of at Chattenden, plus a father figure in a legendary figure at Chattenden, Jock Muir, who was a plant operator mechanics instructor and a legend within the Royal Engineers. Such was the esteem that Jock did his own thing. As a result, he was only a corporal when I first met him. However, with twelve months left, he was promoted to staff sergeant for pension purposes. What a man! I was sad to hear of his demise last year!

At the NAAFI, I was well liked, as I had skinny hands and a good hosepipe. Once, the NAAFI closed, the metal grill came down; no more drink till 18.00, except, my hosepipe and skinny hand could get through the slotted chain bar. I used to attach it to the scrumpy and then the lager and fill the empty glasses the staff had not picked up meanwhile their deserved break. Alice, the manager, could not understand why we were lying steaming drunk and her tanks were empty! I did say I was entrepreneurial; I charged everyone 20p a pint, which went into a local charity fund and then had the hosepipe back on the washing machine meanwhile the evening session began!

Anyway, the high spot of the week at Chattenden was Thursday night; alongside our own NAAFI, we ran our own independent bar due to the urgency to drink and made a small fortune after buying our beer wholesale from the NAAFI. As a result, I used to give reasonably nice-looking girls free drink (brownie points).

I had got myself a nice girlfriend from a place called Snodland, near Gravesend. After spending a weekend with her, I came out of her house to be met by a fat, filthy singer, who had a few big hits 'Big 5', 'Big 7', 'Big 8'. His name was Judge Dread and he said to me, 'I can have her anytime I like!'

This infuriated me that someone could be so blatant; an issued hiding was forthcoming, despite my age and size. Imagine my shock when I got dumped for being cruel?!

I then met a beautiful young WRAC lady and once again fell in love, got engaged, and then again pulled back from the brink; the next time I met Allison, she was a lesbian in the Garrison town of Rheindhalen.

I met a Fifty-nine Commando soldier called Cpl Skip Jones at Chattenden. It was Seventeen Squadron RE Sports Day; however, we decided that prior to the sports, we would go on a run. Skip was in training for selection to the regiment (SAS), so we set off on an eight-mile run at a good pelt; we both came back completely drained. Then, the Seventeen Squadron sergeant major invited us to run in the 5,000 metres, twelve and a half laps of the track. I went out fast, and after four laps, I had already started to lap people; towards the end, I completely ran out of gas and a Seventeen Squadron Scotsman whose surname I forgot, Lennie, pipped me to the line with Skip behind me.

Two weeks later at the Chatham Garrison games, I finished in third place against real athletes in a time of fifteen minutes and one second! It was great time for a boy who was still just eighteen. I remember one of my Chepstow 71b colleagues saying, 'I had no idea you could run like that!' I felt brilliant.

My final defining moments at Chattenden were running the line in the Royal Engineers vs. London All Stars to commemorate the centennial anniversary of the Royal Engineers winning the FA Cup. The All Stars team included Ed *Stewpot* Stewart and one of my rock heroes, Rick Wakeman, who I talked to for a great length of time and was given a great deal of his valuable time, just talking about his individual stuff and not the 'Yes' years.

I loved Chattenden, and rather than go back there, I would jump a year forward a year to the next boxing team; I boxed against Wales and, in my opinion, took apart the Welsh champion, John Wall, only to lose a majority decision. Even Chris Davies came down and said, 'Bob, you were brilliant and was stuffed by the two Welsh judges.'

It made me feel better though I despised losing. At that point, Brian Cherry came over and told me that Fifty-nine Independent Commando Squadron wanted me, and I was getting posted whether I wanted it or not.

Sure enough, RSM Haslett called me and said, 'If you do not want to go, you won't. I will stop it!'

CHAPTER 15

1974 Pre-Fifty-Nine Commando Year

Four Defeats in One Month!

It would be disingenuous of me to write my story and miss out my final months with the Army team. I was the No. 1 choice at lightweight and had three terrific bouts before I left. The first bout was in Leatherhead against London Select; I boxed Moss O'Brien, who went on to become ABA Champion in 1975. Funny thing, his little brother had just joined alongside an intermediate named Steve Holdsworth (now a Eurosport celebrity), whose corner I managed whilst he won the intermediate title. Even though I was boxing that evening, I wanted to assist in any way I could for the betterment and strengthening of our squad.

Anyway, back to Leatherhead; I boxed Moss out of the arena. He hardly touched me in three rounds. Yet for the reason of a poor decision at featherweight, O'Brien got a majority decision and I was really irate about it later, though it was never Moss's fault that there were three blind mice judging. I gave his little brother 'Dog's' abuse when I got back to Aldershot. The reason this is put in is simple; it will lead you on to the funniest story in a boxing ring. Prior to the bouts, we were asked what we would like as prizes. Me, I desperately wanted a new leather protector and duly got it. I loved it and used it in the little sparring I ever did; never saw the point of getting hit for free. It was always on top of my tracksuit bottoms.

My next bout was in the five star Royal Garden Hotel in Mayfair, London, Army vs. London, part 2. Moss was not selected for the bout; I boxed a top man. My routine pre-fight was always the same: I would arrive early, get all my equipment prepared, and weigh in. I would then check the programme to see what bout I was on and calculate my rest period, where I could just go into relaxation mode. (My favourite thought was, and still is, lying after a strenuous workout on the benches at Maida Gym, naked, waiting for a shower and listening to the banter of the team members. It just chills me.) As I said, it takes all sorts! Fifteen minutes before the bout, I had the usual toilet requirements, came out of the toilet, and for some reason, forgot to put my pants on under the protector. I had all my equipment, including my brand new white silk shorts on, combed my hair, put on Vaseline, and donned my red dressing gown. Yes, I looked and felt a million dollars, which was to last all of two minutes. I jumped into the big ring, I took the dressing gown off and a hall full of millionaires burst out laughing. One wag at ringside shouted, 'He has *shat* himself!'

Joe turned me round to look and said, 'You have shit all over your beautiful white shorts.'

That was the one moment in my whole life that I wish I could just vanish. I was so embarrassed yet still had to box. I was not letting these upper class 'silver spooners' think I was a coward. I went on the attack for three rounds; it wasn't the usual me. I was beaten again. I maintain to this very day that I wiped my bum properly, but due to being very hirsute everywhere, it was sweat that caused the stain!

Bout 3 took me to Hartlepool to box the great George Feeney, who I should have boxed whilst at Cove. This was the only other bout in which I took a hiding. I met George and we chatted about the last time we had met each other in Leeds at the NABC Championships. The bout was my nadir, due to assuming I had made it with the 'professional' contract being dangled. The proof of the pudding came in less than one minute; we came out and George threw a jab to my head. I felt not a thing yet was sitting on my now cleaned white shorts. I got up quickly, unhurt; the same scenario happened three times with his next three punches. At no time was I hurt or groggy. The referee could see I was OK, but I said, 'Just call it!'

George had his jab to such precision to me it had a tipping effect. There was no way I was going to win it, so I just gave in, the one and only time I ever did that. George also won European Lightweight Championship and fought Ray 'Boom-Boom' Mancini for the world title.

Bout 4 took me back to Hanley to box against Wales for the third time. This time, the opponent was Charlie Brown, another up-and-coming good fighter. I got into the ring and checked the judges: there were three Welsh ones and two Army ones with a military referee. I looked at Joe and said, 'I need a stoppage to win this.' After my Feeney fight, I just wanted a win for me and no one else. I would swear on a stack of Bibles I boxed really well and again won every round, even dropping him on to his knees in the second round. Guess what? The decision came in and I had lost 3-2. The only thing that cheered me was the raucous amount of booing from the crowd; this went on for a few minutes and slightly delayed the light welterweight clash. I then left immediately for Plymouth to represent Fifty-nine Commando in the Minor Units Final against the para-signallers, who were training at Maida Gym on the other side of the net from the Army squad. I knew my opponent was constantly watching me throughout training and I would smile every time I caught him observing me at Nelson Barracks Gym, only five days after the theft by Brown in Stoke. I needed a win; Brian had been telling everyone just how good I was, and I had not even trained with anyone from the team. I weighed in three pounds under lightweight, boxed poorly, yet still won comfortably. Brian was at a loss. Yet according to the lightweight rankings, I had a good chance of winning the ABA title this year, and all I wanted to do was get Christmas over, go on to take the CSBA title, and win the ABA in early May.

The next morning, I was brought in to meet the outgoing SSM, Geoff Smee, and the incoming one, Steve Pickles, who told me I was going on the next Commando Course at the Citadel, Plymouth, in the first week of January. I was furious as this; they had gone against the agreement to allow me my attempt at the ABA title despite all of the pre-posting promises. I will never forget Steve's words, 'You're a fuckin' soldier now. Get on with it!'

As I said in many chapters, my low self-esteem made me push beyond the boundaries of many of my friends, yet I never seemed to want to close the book on achievements. So yes, I signed up as a soldier in the ABAs and everything else would just have to be put on hold, as I would obviously miss all championships whilst at the Citadel and Lympstone. One thing I did know was that I was not leaving Lympstone without a green lid. Low self-esteem or not, no one could dig deeper into the guts and determination more than me. I could do 100 sit-ups on a forty-five-degree-angled bench and had a resting heartbeat of thirty-eight. I was mentally unstable unfortunately, but I knew that if I kept that mouth shut, I would do well!

CHAPTER 16

The Fifty-Nine Years Commando Course and All

Before I begin, let me say I loved Fifty-nine, though reading this diatribe, you may think 'This guy is off his head,' whereas I know it! I decided not to go home over the Christmas period and stayed at Seaton Barracks, not Crownhill Fort, where I should have been. I had a nice wee girlfriend who was extremely mischievous. After our initial meeting, set up by Brian, I spent a few days at her home. For some reason, I treated her abysmally; however, she stuck to me. I was out running every morning and doing all that was required (I thought) for the All Arms Pre-Commando Course, known as the 'beat up'. I went off beans, whilst with this 'lady'. It was Day 3 of the romance, and she asked me to help her make tea; there were three couples together that day. I refused, so I think she thought, 'I will teach him a lesson!' She got my mate, who will remain nameless, to assist in my place. It was simply beans on toast, hardly difficult, and it tasted fine; however, it transpired she had given my friend oral sex and spat it in the beans. 'Biatch!' That was me finished. I went back to Seaton Barracks that night and never saw her again.

On 5 January 1975, the four-tonner was waiting to take us 'volunteer' victims to the Citadel for a crazy fortnight, where, although fully trained, we thought we did not know our head from our feet. The instructors were asked to give me a hard time as, unbeknownst to me, I had been singled out to take the next course, as the squadron would be in Castle Dillon in Northern Ireland at the end of our Commando Course. This is held at Lympstone, near Exmouth in Devon. Don McMaster or Paul Gilbert and I would always seem to do things first, like taking the shell around the square at triple time or doing the front abseil down a steep wall leading to the tunnel assault course. The camaraderie was absolutely brilliant amongst everyone, artillery or engineer, and from Sapper/Gunner to Captain/Major. So I was in my element telling, no screaming, at captains and majors, having utter disregard for the breed (silver spooners)! We were all a number, nothing more or less. I loved Plymouth, I really did; it is a city steeped in history like no other. The pubs were brilliant, and though the Navy guys (Matelots) did not usually mix in certain drinking establishments, the Royal Marines (Booties) were always out with us or on the doors of nightclubs making extra money. The nightlife was superb, and no one seemed to cheat you.

For the first time, we actually kept our weapons in the room, no ammunition though! This was to let us get used to every part of the self-loading rifle (SLR), which fired 7.62 mm ammunition and was known by us as 'the widowmaker' because when it was fired, it would leave a tiny hole at the front, but turn the target or body over and there was no back left! We were transported to Bickleigh Tarzan course, which really belonged to Forty-two Commando Royal Marines. We were given in-depth instruction on each obstacle, how to manoeuvre the course safely, and then, after having walked it, were run back to the Tarzan Course Car Park, which is part of a natural beauty spot. We were then shown the obstacles on a map and sent off at two-minute intervals to complete this trial of 'mind over matter', everyone to a man passing, because all you could hear between the gasping for breath was each member of our 'new team' encouraging each other over the trials; it was a positive and eye-opening experience for me. I, who in the last three years had boxed individually or set out officer assessment courses, helped get people fit, but all as an individual, though the day I boxed George Feeney, I could have done with major back-up. This was a completely new experience to me, and as everyone had passed well within the time, we were presented with less beat-up beasting for that day only.

Week 2 at the Citadel had arrived; it was test week to decide if you progressed or stayed. The staff did not want people who would come back, having failed. The assault course was first; it began with a zipline down to the start of the course using a wet canvas toggle as your handle. It was freezing, as it was January, but the course, especially the tunnels, were soaking wet, not icy. We manoeuvred through the course with exactly the same camaraderie, willing each other on. I was fine till halfway through the final tunnel; I put my hand in a dead cat's guts. The smell was nauseating. It was there to show that you could expect anything in any tunnel at any time. Nevertheless, I had a time to beat and pushed till I got to the final obstacle: the forty-foot cargo net and back to the starting point. I was stinking of dead cat, almost puking, and the final climb was difficult under normal circumstances, never mind the time of year, etc. I made it just in time, though it was a difficult climb, with wet, sticky, gooey hands. Why, oh why, was I working so hard and being part of a team when I could have deliberately failed, returned to the unit, and gone back to the Army boxing team?

I really had no idea, and now I have no regrets, but being, in my opinion, nailed on to win the ABA lightweight title, it is difficult to understand. I had never in my years met so many dedicated engineers together (skip the Green Lid). They looked out for each other. If they could see you may have a problem, they would do all in their power to alleviate it. Be it a huge blister or a swollen ankle, they would go get ice from the kitchen, not enough time to get things done before inspection; anything, just anything, to be part of a team, which is why when I met these guys after forty years, it really was just like last week, although the mirror did say different!

At the end of the week, no one knew who was going to Lympstone, and we were sent out to say goodbye to the Citadel by running around it in full kit. As we got back in the gates, we were told either 'On the wagon' or 'Try again.' Fortunately, I made the wagon.

We arrived at Lympstone on Monday, 20 January 1975 and were immediately given grief, having to collect a massive amount of equipment at one time and sprint back to the block about 500 metres from the store, always having to stop to pick up equipment we had dropped. I had a Cockney, Corporal Tomlinson, in my ear for nearly nine weeks giving me extra grief, but we, the Citadel boys, had came up with our saying, 'I am a rubber duck, and you cannot crack me,' and we meant it with every fibre of our being. Despite the horrendous weather, the hill with so many rises we called it Heartbreak Hill, of course Lympstone's very own assault course, the regain rope over a freezing cold tank of water, and finally, the estuary where we did the classic mud runs, everything about Lympstone was one step higher than before; I can say with some pride that I may be the only Green Beret actually to fail one part of the course.

Sailors did not volunteer for the course but had to do it to work with 'Booties'. As such, their attitudes stank and they did not care about passing. We got to the famous endurance course where you have to go in teams of four. Again, knowing I was going to be training staff, I was allotted two Matelots and a very quiet gunner as my teammates. We began with poor little me having to start the session. I had to break the ice with my rifle butt and then cross to the other side of the pool, at all times screaming at my teammates to get a move on. We ran up the hill and through two tunnels before meeting the 'water tunnel', which was a nine-foot concrete tunnel, completely submerged.

The drill was simple: You left your weapon on top of the tunnel, one team member would grab you, thrust you down, and ensure he could push you as far as possible by submerging himself. He then pushed you as far as possible whilst the third man, at the other side of the tunnel, would go under and feel for a strap or piece of clothing and pull you out. 'Simple,' I thought. I pushed the first man thoroughly well inside the tunnel, and the sailor on other side got him out, no bother.

I was nominated as Man 2 and prepared for my go; the sailor pushed me down and gave a little push—I was barely in the tunnel and had to use some initiative, or I was in trouble big time. I felt for the tunnel joint and pulled my way forward until the other man could pull me out. I was furious; I pulled out the final man and warned him he was going to get it, as he was my pusher. Anyway, after that, there were a few more obstacles, then a straightforward six miles back to Lympstone in soaking wet equipment, down to the ranges, and firing of five rounds at a target. I think the time allowed was ninety minutes. When we started the run back to camp, I was livid, as the Matelots did not seem to care. I took the weapon from one sailor and the webbing off of the other and attached them to my small frame, screaming at them non-stop through the six miles. On approach to the camp, with 800 metres left, I yelled 'Don't quit!' At that point, I returned their equipment to them and screamed for a final push. We got into camp and fired on the range exactly one minute too late.

I had made the supreme effort, so said in my gobby way, 'F*ck it! Stick the course where the sun does not shine!' Normally, that would be that. However, the officer I/C of our course was a Dutch Marine and had been deliberately following me throughout the course just to see if I could do the job. He walked over and explained to the sergeant major the course of events and demanded I be passed.

It was now a matter of pride for me to do the mud run in the estuary, climb the thirty-feet rope fully equipped, and do the regain. The test is to slide face down out along a horizontal rope, drop your body off, and hang on by the hands. Then you swing back up and wrap your legs around the rope. From there, you manoeuvre yourself back into the face-down position and continue to move the way you were originally going! Only one slight problem: The tank of freezing water was below you and the Booties were determined we were all getting soaked, so they kept us doing regains till we could hold on no longer, and in we went; our equipment and SLR were soaked through. We then had to go back to our block and put on dry clothes, clean our weapons, and be on parade an hour later, immaculately turned out for weapon inspection. Believe me, an hour is not a lot of time to get sorted out, clean and remove the rust from your weapon right down to the firing pin, then go and be inspected. We did as ordered, our weapons were checked, and although you heard the sighs from Corporal Tomlinson, who had the eyesight of a trained sniper, another job was done.

It was Week 9 and one more test stood between us and the coveted Green Beret and dagger shoulder flash. This was a night exercise in a hurricane and a thirty-mile map reading exercise which had to be completed within ten hours. That was carried out on Dartmoor and included many of its worst features. Halfway through the exercise, End-ex was called, as the weather was worse than atrocious. We were ordered to bivouac up and get food down us and then perhaps get three hours' sleep. We didn't require telling twice; within a few minutes, cooking stoves were hissing and the distinctive smell of hexamine blocks filled the air. We then put all our rations (three courses) into one mess tin, mixed it together, and ate it as a stew whilst our other mess tin was filled with water for a hot drink. After our feast, many went to sleep, whilst others, such as Paul Gilbert, Paddy Rainey, and I meticulously gave our weapons a check for rust, etc. I was so glad I had tied a finger stool round the barrel, as no rust was found. The next morning, we were put into teams again, funnily enough the same team as the endurance course. I had the Matelots, who had retaken the endurance course and passed! Paul Gilbert had the 'Galloping Bishop' (Padre) in his team, who did not have to carry a weapon, but had a ten-pound steel shepherd's crook instead. We felt we had done really well, and all of us checked each other's kit for correct fitting, dextrose tablets to give us more energy, and a full water bottle. This time, everything went to plan, and we were all in within the time limit, to be met with a brew and a filled roll.

The next day, we were on the square in our denims and cap comforter. The Marine band was playing, and as we were paraded in front of the staff, the Dutch major would inspect us, then, one by one, take off our cap comforters and fit us with our more-than-deserved green beret. On returning to Crownhill, orders were up as to which troop we were assigned to and where we were going. Some got Malta/Ireland, some got Condor/Ireland, I was posted to Support Troop and the next 'beat-up' instructor!

CHAPTER 17

Fifty-Nine Years, My First Beat-up

Well, this was it, my first beat-up had arrived. I knew no names; I just knew that when they got to Lympstone, everyone I sent was going to pass and feel great about themselves. Among the greats I took through were Tony Dalton, Ian Gorthy, Al Pederson, Ian Pogson, and Les Rutherford. One not so great was Staff Sergeant Cummings from Chepstow; however, this caused me more joy than the rest of them put together. I casually asked if he would like that 'go' now.

He said, 'Not now, maybe later, though!' That cost him thirty sit-ups and press-ups for not calling me Staff or Corporal. This was going to be fun!

I then took them for their first run over the Seaton Barracks Cross-country Course carrying logs. For extra encouragement, I, believe it or not, was carrying a fully fledged bull whip, which I was adept at cracking for effect. Honestly, the Booties on the gate must have thought I was insane. After the forty minutes cross country, they were taken by me to one of the treats of Crownhill: the Moat Run, albeit gently and with plenty of humour thrown in. Down we went. I said, 'Gentlemen, you are lucky. There are only three inches of water. I am sure I can arrange it to be fuller before this fortnight is over!' We jogged round, showing them how to use their mate as a major help over the walls and old house; it was all about teamwork. If they wanted to pass, they did not have to be the best, just give everything they had at all times.

After a few hours, you could see the cream rising to the top; it was then I decided with the rest of my training team (any Fifty-niners who were on rear party) that we were going to be fair, firm, and friendly to *all* on the course. I decided it was not about revenge, more like building a team you could trust. I turned it into a team competition, having Troop 1 and Troop

2 led by Sgt Les Rutherford and S/Sgt Cummings, and we did loads of team building 'games', one of which was rather unique; maybe I will tell of it later, but you would have to sign the official Secrets Act first. We started with thirty individuals, and after Day 1, we were down to twenty-seven.

Day 2: I had the teams in a large circle playing a game with a medicine ball, then got out the ash poles, my weapon of choice used to build arm strength. The pole was clasped in both hands, shoulder length apart, and you had to twist the pole forward for thirty seconds, then backwards every thirty seconds or whenever I shouted 'Change.' I told them when they had enough just to sit down. Now this exercise really does burn the muscles; after two minutes, the guys started to drop out and sit down; some lasted five minutes and sat down. I was getting bored watching Dalton and Pederson going at it. Eventually, at ten minutes, I called a halt, a phenomenal effort! I could not believe what I had witnessed, and then Al Pederson said, 'What is next, Staff?'

I gave everyone a break and told them to be back in thirty minutes, when we would do the Army PT Physical Fitness Assessment, followed by the Battle Fitness Test before lunch. Everyone was back in twenty-five minutes, and I was called into the office by 'Lt Folwell', my nemesis, who said he had been informed by neighbours around 'the Moat' about my choice of words: I had to stop swearing. Great! Day 2 and I had to choose my words carefully. I was very happy with the twenty-seven men left; no complaints. They worked hard, took a joke, and what's more, I liked this group of men.

Day 3 began with a quick run in a fuller moat. It had not rained; I just put a few hundred gallons in that night. Everyone was out of puff, and after a quick breather, I decided on a mud run on the Tamar Estuary. It was two miles downhill all the way; everyone was very comfortable. I then had them enter the mud flats; for demonstration purposes, I also joined in. We did fifty-yard dashes, sit-ups, press-ups, and my favourite, the 'jack-knife', where hands and feet meet at twelve o' clock with only your bum in the mud. I got them out; they were only wearing denims and boots. I broke the news we were going to run all the way back to camp; anyone who got caught walking was going home. It was then that they realised it was now all uphill for two miles on a 1:7 hill. I could see their faces change as the enormity sank in, but told them, 'If you really want this, you will manage it.'. Mind over matter! The corny old: 'I don't mind, and at the moment you really do not matter!' I could see hackles rise; it was having a profound effect on those twenty-seven great sappers. I led the way, and each 'troop' took off a minute apart. I had two 'Fifty-niners' hiding at different points, and I kept running up and down to check on the groups. I could not believe what I was seeing; these guys were giving their all—as if their very lives depended upon it. I felt a massive surge of pride; one even completed with a twisted ankle. 'Mind over matter' got them to the finish. I told them to go rest and get their kit ready; the next day, I was going to start the testing. I was so proud of them all. They got the afternoon off, whilst I and two other members went out in a Land Rover so I could work out a new, final ten-mile test which would make or break them. We went on to Dartmoor, looking for long straight stretches with a few good inclines and no downhill till the finale. We took two hours creating the route, which would end in a nice pub at the top of Bickleigh! Going back to camp, Corporal Ray Ellis, with whom six weeks later I would do the Army show, asked me if I was being fair. I said casually, 'Ray, would you rather see fit happy passes or fit broken failures?'

He replied with a smile and said, 'You sadistic c*nt!'

I had planned the final ten-miler for the last day of the course starting at 6 p.m.: more later.

As you now know, I was extremely proud of this group. From young men just out of training to real men who knew the score, I held a real affinity with Les Rutherford, who was also a diver, and he was to prove to be my big brother when required in Cyprus.

The next day, I introduced weight into their bergens and gave a lesson on foot protection, an absolute must for this type of work. There was loads of banter, which I happily gave and took. After a casual question-and-answer session, they all looked so relaxed and happy. I could not have that, or the next thing I knew, I would be a wimp. I invited them to drop their webbing and bergens at the guardroom. I announced that Troop 1 would do the moat run clockwise, whilst the others went anticlockwise, with a winner's and loser's prize. I had introduced competition into the mix. Les and Dave had the troops at the moat; it is fair to say I have never seen anyone work as hard as these two groups did to win a race. At the midway point where the walls and houses are, I watched them try everything to hold the other group up. These guys were incredible. We were now down to twenty-four, though, as two injured their ankles in the moat. Both teams rose from the moat at about the same time, with Les Rutherford's winning by seconds. The reward was to have the afternoon off and prepare everything for the next day's final ten-mile slog. The losing team were going over the cross-country course with full packs! Fair, firm, friendly . . . no: I changed my mind and asked the veterans to do half their age in press-ups, sit-ups, burpees, and star jumps and the young ones to do double their age for the same exercises, then go get prepared for the final day. Then I and a few of the guys went out on a pub crawl.

The next morning, after fully rehydrating from the night before, I stood in front of these guys and informed them they would do two hours of football and volleyball and then to go and sleep as the final exercise would need everything they had and to ensure they carried their wallets in their bergens! Curiously, they did as required; a four-tonner picked them up from Crownhill at 17.30 and drove them to the 'sadists' ten-miler'. It had to be done in two hours carrying fifty-six pounds and a nine-pound weapon. I was extremely pleased to see everyone checking each other. The veterans were going round the youngsters, ensuring webbing was tight and offering encouragement; it really did feel good. Off we went at the necessary speed to conclude at the pub for 20.00. To this gang, egging each other on, it was definitely not easy, as the short steep inclines caused gaps to appear in the columns, at which I would *scream,* 'You are going to fail!'

Hey, presto! The gaps closed; no doubt they all wanted this. We arrived at the pub ten minutes early, which meant they had completed my tough course in a remarkable one hour and fifty minutes. I ordered, 'Wallets out of packs!' I told them to put their kit on the wagon and to relax, as I was really pleased with them. So they all went in the pub, and for three hours, we bantered, laughed, and drank our fill. Unbeknownst to them, I had a final trick up my sleeve. At 11 p.m., the horn of the vehicle went, and I had twenty-two happy, drunken sappers formed up outside the inn. I shouted, 'You are no longer troops, but individuals. Get on the wagon!' I then blew a whistle. As they ran, the vehicle took off, and the guys were bewildered but chased regardless. I had told the driver to keep the guys in sight and as soon as they were near, to take off and park up at Bickleigh Tarzan Course.

I told the guys I had miscalculated the distance of the march and they had a mile left! Moaning ensued, but they kept going until they reached the Tarzan Course and saw the wagon. At that point, I was obviously drunk as well as immature! I noticed an old yellow Ford Cortina with steamed-up windows. I quietly asked for eight volunteers and for the rest to quietly get on the wagon. All I can say is the earth moved for the people in the car. On my command, 'Hands on—lift up!', my volunteers picked up the car and moved it right into the centre of the car park. At that point, we got on to the wagon and drove back to camp, where everyone was passed and had a weekend to get their kit together and make me feel proud at the Citadel, as I was going with them. To the poor couple, I apologise and really, really hope you saw the funny side of it!

CHAPTER 18

The Citadel Instructor, Army Show, and Condor Troop

I proudly arrived at the Citadel to help the best commando training team in the world, headed by Corporal 'Dickie' Bird. I had got the twenty-two remaining engineers from my thirty starters and expected all twenty-two to go to Lympstone and have them come back with the green beret. I was so proud of the guys and the efforts they gave me. I was asked by the training team about my 'ten-miler escapade'. My simple answer was, 'We must always be prepared, regardless of the circumstances.' Although I was a trained assistant PTI, this to me was a more fulfilling experience: working with guys who had ambition and the balls to put in what was required. Every night at about 17.30, a Land Rover would pick me up from the guardroom. As we usually finished for the day at 17.00, I would spend half an hour in the guardroom bantering with the Regimental Police and also a very special man, Sergeant 'Punchy' Murray. It was fun and a good finish to my day.

The sappers had settled in and took the first day in their stride, with two laps of the Citadel and an introduction to the Assault Course with Weapons; it certainly brought back memories for me! It is sufficient for me to say that from the twenty-two men who started at the Citadel, three got injured, but nineteen went on to Lympstone and all came back badged, with one member, Tony Dalton, winning the commando medal for best soldier on the course.

I knew that the Army Show Display Team was to be five of the rear party, as the squadron were still in Ireland. I only remember that Ray Ellis led our team and we were joined by five members of Nine Independent

Parachute Squadron RE to be the display team. We had a very tall tower built by Three Training Regiment, and we all got together to decide who would do which manoeuvre. There was a high zipline on which the rope tricks would be performed and a lower line for children to be given the opportunity of sitting and feeling the speed before being stopped. There were different rope tricks.

1) The Front Angel . . . Man lies on top of the rope with one leg dangling and arms outstretched, takes off down the incline head first, and when nearing the end, he simply grabs the rope and automatically brakes.
2) The Back Angel . . . Exactly the same as above except you go feet first, and someone shouts, 'Brake!'
3) The Peel Off . . . Candidate acts afraid of doing his 'first' front angel, refuses to go. He then starts off slowly going down the rope, and after about ten seconds, he screams and falls off, with the crowd in shock. However, he is attached to the rope by a smaller rope and carabineer attached to his ankle. Note: The commando who did that was a Scotsman called Billy; with the twisting effect and torque, his ankle was badly bruised. However, Billy said, 'No point in us all having a bad ankle. I will just carry on.' It took some bottle to know your ankle was going to get sorer with eight more shows.
4) Front Abseil . . . Walk or run down tower to halfway, step over the rope, effectively tying yourself up, and then just reach out with the abseil rope bearing your weight.

It was all good fun, and after we finished our three shows, we would go to the beer tent and relax, playing drinking games. We had a good laugh for the first two days and were looking forward to our final session on Sunday and travelling back to Plymouth. Our final show was completed successfully, and we headed to the bar after taking down all our own equipment. We retired to the bar for the final time, and everyone ordered a round, as it was known the bar would close earlier. We were two pints through our tableful, when the Military Police told us to get out; we refused, so the policeman called for back-up in the shape of mounted policemen. A fracas occurred and a member of Nine Squadron must have watched *Blazing Saddles* prior to the event and punched the horse. From what I understand, that was game over; we all left the tent with the punching corporal being detained in custody, reduced to the rank of sapper and a £250 vet bill.

After the course, I expected to go back and prepare the ground for our next beat-up; however, I was sent to Arbroath to join Condor Troop, who worked alongside Forty-five Commando. In a way, I was happy being only twenty miles from home; I could see civilian friends whenever I had a few hours, had I wanted to. I was at Condor for two days when the first assignment came in. We were to build a swing bridge over the River Findhorn for the World Orienteering Championships, then take it down and ship all the equipment back to Condor, as it was on private ground and the owner had no wish for permanence, due to the opportunities it would offer salmon poachers. The site was very remote and, to put it mildly, the run down through the forest with the equipment was hairy. All was good in other respects, as we stayed as a troop at RAF Kinloss, just twenty miles away. The food was excellent and the facilities were second to none. For a fleeting moment, I wished I was RAF! We competed with the RAF lads at five-a-side football, volleyball, and even played squash, but our desire to be winners meant we sometimes disregarded the rules.

However, it was obvious we were respected, and life was good. I spent the first night on guard at the river; it was just a simple check of equipment and I had plenty to eat, but the incessant roaring of the Findhorn in spate stopped me getting any sleep. I was still fairly alert, had a wee swim in the morning, and ablutions were completed before Bob Munro, Al Pederson, and big Don McMaster arrived in the Land Rover with a special treat of a full breakfast for me. The four-tonner arrived ten minutes later and the work began. Don was checking out the salmon jumping and how to catch them, while Corporal 'Mac' McDonald had given us our teams and tasks on the build. We had the narrow swing bridge built and tested within a week and went back to Condor until the deconstruction was to take place some three weeks later. We went out on the lash in Arbroath, and I was surprised to see the Ford brothers and George Ferry, all from the boxing community I had grown up amongst, running most of the nightclub doors, which meant me and my mates were getting in without a hitch. Unfortunately, this was the beginning of the end for me.

We went to the Station Hotel, a good hostelry, for a few drinks, and there were very few in. I was attracted to a young woman sitting with an old lady and asked them if they would like to join our company. They came across and joined us, and we were bantering with them. It turned out the blonde youngster was seventeen and was employed as the ladies' assistant. It was obvious to a blind man that she was attracted to Mac, but I, remember, was a winner and I wanted this blonde 'goddess' and I was going to get her—what a bloody idiot! Dorothy was from Cupar in Fife but lived in Dunshelt, Auchtermuchty, and was there for an early summer break.

Mac was not interested in what he called 'smally girls' (young and immature) and made this clear, so yes, I was in there pitching my best lines. We met them, us as a group, for the next two days, and everyone enjoyed each other's company.

Dorothy then said, 'Why don't you come over to Cupar the next weekend you are off?'

I automatically said yes. I got her phone number, and for seven days, I phoned religiously, every night bantering and joking and spending a fortune on phone calls, thinking I was fabulous. The following Friday, I made my way to Cupar with a small weekend bag. I was met at the train station and taken to meet Dorothy's parents and then went out to a few pubs where she had many friends; yes, I was enjoying their jokes, and overall, they were nice people. We then went for a Chinese meal and made our way back to her house. I had my 'slug' with me and quickly nodded off, only to be roused, not thirty minutes later, by an apparition in white. She took the lead and we made love for the first time. After a quick cuddle, she went back to her own bed. Oops! Here we go again; I was in love.

One incident I had worried about all my time was that we went up to Ballachullish to get used to the heavy snow conditions. We stayed in the para hut. Ian Pogson volunteered to come with me up Aanoch Mhor; when we reached the top, it was more or less a whiteout and a narrow glacier ridge. Ian and I stopped and could not work out where we were. I *bottled* it and actually cried.

Ian, quick as a flash, said to me, 'Bob, who is the craphat here?' in a not too sarcastic manner. It sorted me out; we tracked back and realised if we went down on a north-west tangent, we would come to the main road and then it was just a three-mile stroll back to the hut. As far as I am aware, Ian told no one, as I heard no sarcasm from anyone, and let's face it: How easy would it be to take the mickey out of a panicking beat-up instructor!

CHAPTER 19

Fifty-Nine Cdo RE, the Defining Year

As I have already said, stupidity regarding women was always going to be my downfall. I had no idea that victims tend to think terms of endearment, even made jokingly, become an invisible string to assist in tying together a broken heart! Was I ever going to learn? Because of extreme low self-esteem issues, I saw myself as an ugly person (yet looking at new pictures from then, I know this was not the case) who should grab anybody who liked me. It was August 1976, I was twenty-one, and so in my mind, it was marrying age. So the next weekend, I went and bought a ring and surprised Dorothy whilst she was in Dunshelt: Her employer was over the moon. So I think she went along with it to please her and we set a date of 1 October; just eight short weeks away. She met both my grandparents and my mum, who said it was obviously no love match. However, I refused to listen, as I should have, and went on with the planning at weekends after working at Condor all week. I could even begin to hear her impatience on my never-ending phone calls. It was so bad I was becoming unstable and was due to return to the Army team mid-October, being told I was still the Number 1 despite Steve Holdsworth winning the CSBA title. Anyway, as we got near our marriage date, she got cold feet and wanted to call it off—she just was not sure. Me, being the guy looking for love, went to see her, and after two hours of begging and pleading, it was back on. Looking back, it was stupidity in the extreme. Married quarters were arranged quickly, and she got an evening job, just as well it was not as a cook! My first meal I will never forget; it was macaroni and cheese; it looked fine but she had not cooked the macaroni. Already, after just a few weeks, it was chaos; she would get in late from her job in a chip shop. She wanted a housewarming party, aiming to please, then she suggested swapping partners, yet already knew I was insanely jealous. She then asked for a differing colour scheme in the quarters, which had to be returned to original before handover. However, me, being eager to please, I did as asked though the people from military housing were just like the East German military 'Stasi!'

When I returned to the Army team in October, it felt surreal, as I went straight to Joe Kiernan's home and said I was giving up boxing and was returning to Plymouth. Joe told me to think about it for a day or two; however, I was adamant: I was going back to Plymouth. Looking back from my position now, it was down to a complete mistrust in Dorothy.

One night, she went out with some friends she had made across the road, whilst I sat and watched TV. The next morning, Brian told me he had seen her in a club with the older guy, who just happened to live as a lodger across the road with her friend. I now know why she went across so often; when she finished work that night, I asked her about it and she said nothing. Meanwhile, I was in training with the Fifty-nine boxing team for our second consecutive Minor Unit Championship final which was now but four days away.

I was fit on weight, but there was no spark in me, as I was constantly worrying what she was up to. I got home one night, and she was not there, neither were any of her belongings. I was walking on eggshells, sitting weeping like a small child. I then went across to her friend's, got in the door illegally with fury on my face, I grabbed hold of the lover, head-butted him, and gave him a bit of a hiding whilst shouting, 'Where is she?' He said she had gone home, so I had a simple choice: wait two more days, box, then go after her or just go at that moment!

I took the illogical choice and took off for Cupar to find her. I ran out of the house with literally pennies in my pocket and thumbed a lift to Cupar. The journey was done in ten hours. I got there, but Dorothy was hiding in Blantyre. Her parents gave me the address, so I went across Scotland to find her. I knew I would not have long, as I was boxing in two days. After meeting her, she said she would try again. So stupid me went to the Army Careers Office and got two warrants to get back, which would have to be paid for. To make things even worse, he relegated me, and put in the reserve Terry McGiveron in and he was hammered; if the team had been beaten, it would have been my fault.

It all seems insane and stupid now. When I returned to Crownhill, the new OC, Major Fields, immediately busted me to sapper and fined me £60 on top of the travel warrants. So now we were skint and using her meagre wages to buy the cheapest food: Knorr Square-shaped soup etc., making things even more strained!

People lacking in self-esteem are likely to mistakenly believe that sex—not their personality—is their only way of winning the love they desperately need. They fall for the horrible lie that their only chance of receiving even an illusion of the love they crave is to yield to sexual advances. This makes them highly vulnerable. So intense is the pressure that they need far superior self-control than other people need in order to remain sexually pure.

Moreover, abuse survivors are strongly tempted to accept the lie that because they have been mistreated before, they have little purity left to protect. If technology had moved forward to the point that it is now, then I would have already learnt that I was suffering mental trauma. The peace was to last less than two weeks and she ran away again; this time, with the same lover who owned a bookshop in an ancient part of Plymouth. I just went and poured a gallon of water through the shop door with a final warning note. I knew it was over, so I just went to hand the keys to the quarters back and was told to be there the next morning for the 'Stasi' inspection. I cleaned everything I possibly could, but there was no way I could paint it or indeed finish the new painting I had started. I failed the inspection and had to go see the adjutant, Lt Folwell. He gave me a right mouthful and said I would have to pay for the painting and cleaning to be done for me. Besides which, he said, 'Everyone knows you married a tart!'

At this, I lost it and attacked the adjutant with gusto, actually wrapping the wire of the phone around his neck. He screamed like a stuck pig, and both members of the Pay Corps sitting in the next office had to rush in and peel me off him. I knew he was correct, but as the adjutant, he should have known better! I was charged within an hour and was back in front of Major Field and was sentenced to twenty-eight days' jail and received a three-month warning, which meant if I did anything wrong, I was out of the Army; he also put me on a transfer list to move me out! I had made the worst mistake ever. I would definitely come to regret a few instant decisions.

As you know, I had gotten to know Punchy Murray very well whilst at the Citadel. So while the rest of the RP staff were about, he gave me hell; when alone though, it was different. He would bring in a paper for me and even placed a bet for me on a horse. It was the first day of the flat at Doncaster and its name was 'Rollaston'; it romped home at 20/1 with my last £1 on it. I was given PT by the training staff, and it was difficult, but I was better than most of them, so hardly worked up a sweat. On leaving the Citadel, Punchy came and gave me a ticket for a night out to see the

Tom Robinson Band in a nightclub. I had my £20 from my horse win, so I went out; whilst in jail, you get no pay, so I really needed the cash. I was chatted up by a gay man and realised what type of band this was when they belted out their anthem, 'Sing If You're Glad to Be Gay!' I was getting out of there sharpish.

I was then informed that the ex-missus had slept with Alex Higgins, the snooker player, while she was working in the hotel trade: I was raging! Fortunately, the next day, I was informed I was leaving for Cyprus on advance party—probably for my own good!

Prior to that, I had moved back in with the guys, who really did try to lift me. I was ordered as a sapper to take charge of the sports store and take a PT class every morning for the support troop. I remember getting up in the morning, grabbing a pair of denims; they had no buttons? So I got out another pair; again no buttons. She had taken all the buttons up for spite! I got a safety pin and attached it to my denims so they looked closed. I took the class. It was OC Adjutant Pay Office Clerks, etc. I was very aware of my shit drills as regards my kit. So that no one noticed, I gave them no time to look at me except when I was demonstrating an exercise. I got away with it, and everyone was shattered. It was at that point, the OC said that as sports store man/Sapper PTI, it would also be my job to wash, dry, and iron all the squadron strips. I had been round the block by then and knew this was a real piss take. Really, everywhere else I had been, strips were sent to laundries to be washed, dried, and ironed. The machine was a really old twin tub; they wanted rid of me; of that, I was extremely sure!

CHAPTER 20

Cyprus and It's All Over

I arrived at RAF Brize Norton the next day, not knowing this was my last month in the forces. I was excited, as I had never flown in a Hercules, and the guys were all kidding me. It was comfortable, quiet, and had plenty of room. There may have been room if we didn't have all the squadron equipment aboard. We flew in this noise bucket for seven hours and arrived at Larnaca totally knackered. You have to remember, this was pre iPod and earphone days. I had tinnitus for three days afterwards. I was still in a massive hole of depression over Dorothy, and I nearly always felt like crying. Hey! I was a commando; it was time to man up and just get to work. Bloody hell! We did not even have a medical centre where I could be diagnosed as mentally ill, not that it would have made any difference; there was no mental health treatment that would have worked on me, and the minute you had a mental issue, you were finished as far as Fifty-nine was concerned.

We left Larnaca and went straight to the campsite via a short stop in beautiful, glorious Paphos (pre-tourism) for refreshments. The Cypriots knew how to keep you thirsty: On top of the bars were plates of carrot wedges soaked in lemon juice and peanuts well salted. I could have happily gone AWOL and stayed there forever; it really was a beautiful place with untouched splendour and stunning architecture.

We left after an hour and set out for base camp, getting it set up and noted at the end of the track, about three miles away, was a café. Once everything was done: tented village up, etc., a couple of guys volunteered to stay. They wanted to stay and dive in the azure blue, warm Mediterranean Sea, while the rest of us wanted food and drink without having to cook. We drove back to the café to find it was owned by a Cypriot called, of all things, Stelios McDonald. He was very astute; we ate merrily and drank heavily; the bill was zero. Stelios was no mug, though; there was not a day in the next twenty that he did not arrive on site for petrol, simulating the need by putting a syphon to his mouth and sucking. At first, while the squadron had not arrived, it was no problem; then, when everyone arrived, it was just a headache!

When the squadron arrived, work began in earnest; each troop had a different job. I was in support troop and so was basically a dogsbody doing anything and everything. After fourteen days on site, there was a change; I went back to Dhekelia, where we shared an engineer squadron's barracks for some rest and recuperation for a week. I was still immensely frail and having talked to the Padre on many occasions, found solace in Ouzo, cheap brandy and lager in copious unhealthy amounts. I was doing silly things. One day, I conked out on a low wall outside the barracks. When I woke about three hours later, I was red raw from the sun, sober, and with the biggest black-and-blue nose I had ever seen. I was on complete self-destruct; this was to culminate in just a few hours' time. I had found out the officers were using the NAAFI club for a private function, and I was livid that our club had been taken and given to them. Not just that, the band were of far superior quality to anything we other ranks had ever got. They had a swarthy Cypriot doorman. I was going in and he was not stopping me. So after a few sherryies and brandies, I was ready to object. I walked past the doorman; he put his left arm on my shoulder, and I right-hooked him to the point of the chin: He landed face down. As I walked drunkenly up the stairs, a major with a plummy voice put his hand on my shoulder and asked me nicely to leave, as it was a 'private function'. He was then doubled over by my hook to his body.

Within three minutes, I was in the back of a Land Rover, heading for the jail of the Irish Rangers. When they got me inside, the huge Provost sergeant came in the cell and gave me a hiding; I was too pissed to fight back. The next morning, he came in to see me, only for me to slam the door when he entered the cell. Quietly and firmly, I asked him if he fancied a go with the wee boy now he was sober. You have to remember, I was totally unstable, so I booted him in the balls and said, 'Quits!' Within two hours, I was charged again on three counts of assault. I was given fourteen days' jail, suspended until we got back to Plymouth, plus a discharge. The squadron worked hard to get the doorman to drop his charge with the civilian police by explaining my last few months. I was sent to Limassol, where another troop were having real fun water-skiing and sunbathing and generally enjoying the beautiful tunnel beach. I was told by Drew, who had not talked to me for a while, that Dorothy was back in Plymouth and had borrowed hundreds of pounds from his very nice girlfriend Liz and had not paid it back. I assured him I knew nothing of this; however, it was another load placed on my back. An hour later, I was sitting on a bed crying like a baby. Somebody called for SSM Steve Pickles, who listened to me for ten minutes, then decided to start my jail sentence at that point, as I was a danger to myself, verging on suicide according to him. I was taken to a Green Jackets' prison. I was shocked on arrival to see a coloured soldier wearing only underwear chained up in a corrugated shed. His crime was being caught on an escape-and-evasion exercise! Heck, what were they going to try on me? It was six days before our trip back to Plymouth.

I instantly started to limp, saying I had hurt my ankle whilst taking revenge. They were not going to be fooled though. As far as they were concerned, I would leave Cyprus having learnt a valuable life lesson—yeah right! I demanded a doctor, who came thinking I was 'at it'. I was. He took my right boot off and my right ankle was heavily swollen; it had been that way since I damaged all the ligaments at Cove—swollen but no pain. Every time the doctor touched it, I would moan; he was agreeable to light duties for six days to rest my ankle. So there were no rapid drills, meals were brought into my cell, and I generally took the piss. On the sixth day, I was transported to Akrotiri in handcuffs to fly back to Brize Norton. We flew by jet this time, quiet and you could hear yourself think. Some of the guys came back with me and talked encouragingly; others completely blanked me. I had let them, and myself, down. When the jet landed, I was first off, with a military police escort the 200 miles back to Plymouth, still in handcuffs. We arrived, I continued to limp; I was not doing anything I didn't have to (with the travelling I had only six days left). The PTI at the Citadel was the same one who used to assist me with the 'Potential Officer Courses' at Chattenden. He attempted to make me do every exercise, however, as I was still 'limping', there was not much he could do. I said to him, 'I will do any stomach exercise you want, and if I can beat you by at least a minute in endurance, or twenty in number, then our PT sessions are over.' He agreed and picked the jackknife. I could do them for hours after all my years with the Army team. He lost and PT was concluded. So right away, I began writing letters for some work. Punchy Murray came in and talked as a friend, telling me to think about things and seek redress to stay in the Army; he even promised to be my advocate. There I was, twenty-one going on twelve. I had a lot to learn and the big bad world was going do that, whether I liked it or not. Even on my last day in jail, two days before returning to the big bad world, Punchy almost pleaded with me, saying, 'There will come a day, and not too far away, when you mature. You will realise just what you have thrown away!' How right he was going to be!

The next day, I got back to Seaton Barracks, only to be ordered that I had to go to the squadron dance that evening. I didn't want to go, but hey, it was a chance to say goodbye to those guys who had stuck by me. I got to the dance, bought a drink, and was drinking it, when SSM Pickles spotted me and walked over to me. He was hurtful in the extreme, telling me to keep well away from him and not 'to cry on his shoulder'. I was absolutely livid; I had done my time in nick. I told him to f*ck off, immediately left the dance, and went back to my room hurt and upset; what a fabulous final night with the squadron!

The following morning at 09.00, I had to hand in my kit, and to my total astonishment, they took absolutely everything back, including my much coveted and prized green beret. I then went to the Pay Office to get my final wages in cash; I still owed £300 in fines and cleaning, so had not a single penny to collect. There I was, with my suitcase of everything I owned dumped unceremoniously by Land Rover at Plymouth Station. As I got on to the platform, I heard, 'Mr Curran?'

I said, 'Yes, what do you want?'

He was from the Rhodesian Army and there and then offered me a job. Now, I was immature and stupid, however, I was not mad; no way was I going to die in the heat of Angola as more or less a vigilante!

I had my red service book and couldn't believe my report said this man is super fit and gives a 'fair' physical training lesson. I also had behaviour as fair, despite only being charged for stupid things prior to getting married, which ruined my Fifty-nine career. So no way was I going to be a fireman, which had been my plan; my life had a few kickings to give me yet. So the Red Book was discarded out of a train window round about Exeter. I really was a very, very angry young man!

CHAPTER 21

Going Home To What?

It was roughly 21.00 hours when I saw Dundee from the Fife side of the Tay Bridge. I, this time, did not feel the usual swell of pride and euphoria when I saw Dundee, in all its glory. All I felt was great trepidation. I had phoned my Uncle Frank from Plymouth; he picked me up from the railway station and brought me to his home for a couple of nights until I could sort my head out. He had 3 young children, and had no space but fitted me in on a couch until I got some money and housing fixed up. It was not at all easy, and Dundee Council said I had no right to any housing so would have to find myself something else. Franks wife did not like me, so after 3 days I left and went to see my Mum, who still lived amazingly frugally, and in complete poverty. She lived in a flat, above a bookmaker, and you could hear every race being talked through all day, and never had any peace. By now I was so down I had not shaved or washed for a week, and must have stunk a bit. I had gone to sign on for unemployment benefit, only to be told this would be refused for 6 weeks as I had been sacked. You do not have an option, civilians would never understand the things I had been through.

I was given a card to go to the DSS the next day. I arrived early; you took a ticket, and sat, and sat, and sat some more, until your number was called. It was then you went and sat in front of a rude young civil servant possibly just out of school, giving your details and being asked all sorts of designative un-needed questions. Of course, as you can imagine, I was losing the plot. Interrogation over, I then went and saw a Doctor as I had broken out in a horrid itchy rash called Lichen Planus, which is an auto immune disease causing an increasingly itchy rash. It can be caused by coming into contact with certain chemicals or CS Gas which I had used quite often for

113

respirator testing drills. The specialist I saw in September 1977 reckons it had to be something I came into contact with whilst in the military as this disease does not start alone. Over the last year I have (had?) suffered umpteen reoccurrences of this disease, and every doctor I saw told me it was Scabies and thus more bathing and painting your body all over. My new doctor asked if the previous doctors had ever checked my notes. It was there, in the notes, clear as day.

I was lucky enough to get a job in a firm called Dundee Fabrics, making and inspecting Corduroy. The money wasn't fantastic and I was very clearly unhappy. I had not been near anyone of the opposite sex for months as I had lost all trust. My mum had a boyfriend called Larry Devlin who was gentle as a lamb, but an alcoholic. His son, also Larry, was ages with me and lived just up the road. So I was introduced, Larry was funny and witty, but heading for drug addiction at a rapid pace. I had not so much as smoked a cigarette, and was still out running in the morning. He lived with his girlfriend in a flat which was to become mine in a short time. They were smoking dope, and after plenty refusals I eventually shared a joint. After 3 hours of this I was out of it, although I kept saying "Nothing is happening". The other 2 were giggling their heads off, and said I would sleep well!! I certainly did, but was up from Mums single bed in the living room early and away to work, managing the boring laborious work without even thinking!!

I was now off the rails completely, drinking, smoking dope, and selling corduroy dumped out of the back window before shift end: about 60-100 metres a week, explaining why half of Dundee had corduroy curtains. Every Friday without fail I would finish my shift and have a taxi to take me into town, and go first to the Breadalbane Arms known locally as "THE BREAD", get some dope then off to the Students Union. Flog my Corduroy simply and have a great night listening to fantastic bands, and once I had my own flat I would without even thinking, have a party till the early hours: 3-4 a, destroying my neighbours. Meanwhile I was knocking off my bullies' one at a time, but felt no real satisfaction: perhaps because deep down I knew I was better than any of them. Word got around and Tommy Rollo, who I had boxed in my earlier life, had asked more if I would do some dealing after work in "The Bread". I said yes as I got a quarter ounce for every 3 ounces I sold. At that time my musical taste was mainly rock so I ran discos there too. People knew me and knew where to come to buy Hashish which I stored in my Album box. A quarter ounce is approximately 7.25 grams, and I would pare off some for myself from every deal. In the end Tommy was being called "5 Gram Tam".

Mixing with the wrong crowd was simple; however I was very wary of smack (Heroin) dealers. Funny thing was, whilst doing discos and dope I was drawing in women again and having a "fun" time. I then began buying and selling "Blues" which were a blue, amphetamine based pill. They were selling really fast, and I got a taste for them. Some nights I was swallowing up to 30 of these a night, which had the effect of making it difficult to find your manhood, never mind use it, except for urinating.

It was making me oh so miserable, I was still working split shifts and not coping with people bothering me or taking the piss, I was just not a nice person. I had pushed the self-destruct button as have many ex-soldiers who are living on couches, or floors of mates. I then found an odd girl: she was funny, artistic, and generally good fun. I moved in with her to get away from the wildest track. Moira was an amphetamine (upper) user and Mandrax (mandies) used to allow her to sleep. So here I was taking dope, amphetamine and mandies just to survive a day. Moira was one of the world's true fun lovers; you could have blown me over when she eventually told me she was a Mormon. I was not worried as long as she stayed fun: once again I was in love.

We went to visit my grandparents who were still living in the same house in Dryburgh. They liked her and she liked them. We used to have a giggle and a laugh about everything, but my other addiction, gambling had come back to the fore. Addie used to like a punt at weekends and I would take it down the bookies, and then gamble big, losing hundreds and not worrying as I was still working. We then began experimenting with Heroin. I injected once and knew immediately I could not ever do that again, so began snorting Cocaine and swallowing LSD and going to the bingo where Moira was working. It was really, really, funny watching numbers jump at you, and I even won a few games tripping. I had decided that even as a junkie, I would never go robbing to get a hit (corduroy apart). One day I received a large shipment of Amphetamine, about 2 ounces or 56 grams, and had put it into .5 g and 1g bags—all slightly light, so I had my freebie. It was good stuff and I hid the rest until after work. I got home and the drug had gone along with my rare albums. It was very fortunate for me as I was in for just ten minutes when my door was caved in and 6 police were in with a dog, searching for what they knew I had. I was handcuffed to the chair, they were meticulous, ransacking every room, and leaving it for me to clear up. They were finished but had found zero, and told me there was 2 sets of known dealer fingerprints. I asked how they could tell that, they told me and to stir it up gave me the names.

I decided to wait a few days as it was fairly obvious they would tail me for a day or so. I then went to the first man's home, was invited in, and immediately saw my rare albums. I asked no more questions; I had my right arm around his throat asking where my "stash" was. He said "I have half but have sold the rest". Raging was not quite how I was feeling. I told him I would meet him in 2 days for my money and I took the rest of the stash. Funny, I was getting really nasty; I had never used a weapon except my fists, when the strangest incident I could ever have contemplated occurred!

Myself and Moira were watching television and were both "straight", when the door went, two well dressed men in their 30's were at the door asking if they could speak to Moira. I invited them in and after a few minutes' preliminaries, they got to the nitty gritty. As I said earlier, Moira was a Mormon or Latter Day Saint, and was told she would be excommunicated because her life standards were not in harmony. Now, ordinarily I would have immediately evicted them: through the top floor window of Moira's Tenement. However something strange happened, I felt relaxed and actually said "Moira if keeping your membership means so much to you take the Bishops invite, get clean!". This meant us getting away from there, living out in the country with my family, until we could get legally married: I was still waiting on my decree absolute. Anyway 2 hours later the Bishop returned with a van, and moved everything to Auchterhouse, 7 miles from Dundee and well away from trouble. I was working the night shift at the time anyway. We met for a few hours at weekends, but by this time my jealousy had returned. She would not answer the phone, then I was told about Polygamy (which ended 120 years before) and questioned the bishop as to what his intentions were, looking back this was really stupid. He said to me "I have made you an appointment to get you clean, meet with our missionaries, who will help" I said "Ok".

I, for some unknown reason, turned up at church that Sunday, dressed in full denims and boots and looked very much the "nigger in the woodpile!" I had moved out of Beechwood and in with my Grandparents, this would work out far cheaper than running a home with one wage. It was a freezing winter and the snow was piled deep. I was asked to go meet the missionaries at their flat. I arrived, cold, miserable, and angry at having to leave my grandparents house and walk across town about 3 miles in knee deep snow. Public transport was off for a whole week in the winter of 1980. Anyway, I warmed myself by their small one bar fire and they started teaching me their beliefs—somehow it interested me. I remember leaving their flat for the walk back to a night shift in my new job, making Tachographs, to meet new legislation brought in during 1979. Feeling a million dollars I walked straight to work my night shift. I was still using but no longer dealing.

Everything was going fine until one Saturday when, whilst my Grandparents were arguing, my Grandad got up and punched my Gran, who by now had dementia. Never in a month of Sundays was I having this. I got up and threw a 3inch right hook to his head: bursting open his eyebrow and knocking him down. He was totally shocked! Of course, that was me homeless again, but striving hard to put my life back on track. I had had 3 overdoses, and did not want a fourth by going back to Mums house in Benvie Road. I had no choice, within 30 minutes Frank was at my house raging, I just laughed and explained the true story. He then calmed down, but the thought of Frank having a go had me giggling. Moira heard about this, that was us finished! I entered emergency council housing on the Monday as I now had a work record. I explained I could lose my home due to having no address. 3 days later I had my first council accommodation, I was in my own home: 5C, Troon Court, Ardler. Rent was not heavy; I could still indulge myself until such a time as the missionaries caught up with me, which would happen soon. I joined the Ardler Community Centre and was asked, with my specialities, if I could take a club 2 hours a week at £17 an hour. I said yes there and then. It was a 7-11 year old club, where I had 3 smaller groups running for fitness, football, arts and crafts. I got on well with the kids and they seemed to like me. On top it was extra cash on top of my weekly wage. Yes, from my point of view, things were improving since my horrific start, to civilian life after leaving the Commando Forces.

CHAPTER 22

The Saving Grace

I had a few opportunities to turn my life around before moving to Ardler. I was taking tough-bred teenagers from Beechwood out towards Edzell for a week's camp to teach them about the great outdoors. I put up two cables across the river, teaching traversing and regaining on the cables. There was a twenty-metre gap between the boys' and girls' camps, and they knew fraternisation was not an option with this mad, mental commando. They were taught camp craft: building fires, cooking skills, and my favourite two, night vision and how sound travels at night. This was a big help regarding the fraternisation rule. I left the female adult and an assistant with a set of instructions of what noises to make on seeing my torchlight. We were on top of a hill looking down on the camp. I asked everyone for silence and then asked what they could see. They spouted a plethora of good observations. I then told them they could see these things as the eye had rods and cones, which worked differently. One by one, I shone a torch in their eyes and asked what they could see. The answer in all cases was nothing. I then blew a whistle, which was a signal for the camp party to follow out my instructions. I had asked for five definitive sounds to be made on the torch signal: from coughing, chopping wood, speaking to her assistant in a normal voice, to pouring water into the river, and finally, striking a match. I instructed the youths to lie back and close their eyes and tell me what they could hear a mile from camp. Each and every person on the top of the hill picked up every sound; they were flabbergasted and amazed, especially with the striking match. I then explained this could really only be done in the quiet of the countryside; it was then they got up and could all see with clarity again, picking out new details such as satellites in the sky. I was happy and I knew the youths were too. There was absolutely no misbehaviour and everybody had enjoyed the week, most especially that night exercise!

I was becoming happier and decided to go box again. I went to a club in Lochee, as I was still only twenty-three. I gave my body a real beasting, doing many, many hill runs as my road to fitness, alongside the usual bag work, circuit training, and sparring. I was again fit and boxed nine times in the Open Class, losing seven to boxers who would not have been entitled to spar with me a few years before. I was still good enough to box for Scotland, getting two caps against Ireland, winning one fight. The funniest thing for me was when I turned up at Dundee's top hotel to watch Scotland vs. RAF. The airman lightweight had gone missing; I was asked to represent the RAF and boxed a good friend, Dougie Reid from Perth; it was a cracker of a bout and Dougie pipped me. The officer in charge of the RAF team recognised me and asked me if I fancied joining up again in the RAF. I jumped at the opportunity, after explaining my full circumstances.

He said confidently, 'Don't worry. I can sort that!'

I went to Careers Office next morning, as I was now adult and knew I could do well. The careers officer made a few calls and said that with my abilities, it would be no problem. If I went back the following day, it should all be sorted out. Excitedly, I was looking to a future and returned the following day in good spirits. As soon as I walked into the office, I knew it was off. I have no idea why; no one would tell me. I suspect it was either the fair Red Book, which I had thrown away, or perhaps a police check had me down as a drug user. Whatever it was, it didn't really matter; it was a bitter blow!

I started back on drugs, as I was sad and depressed, when I had a knock on my Ardler door from Mormon Missionaries. They were young, sincere boys, and I invited them in. I do not intend to say anything derogatory or blasphemous about the Church, which I joined in April 1981, just less than four years out of the Army. I was taught to pray, not just words but like this book, from the heart. There is no doubt at all they have saved my life.

As I said, up till then, I had overdosed three times and hand on heart can tell you that each and every one of my friends and acquaintances from that stage are now dead, in every case, through Aids, which hit Dundee in the summer of 1981, and the first death was a very good friend, Graham Carlin, known as Garlic. RIP, Garlic.

Due to Church involvement, the drugs were gone until I had an accident at work on 31 August 1991, damaging my back to the point I was in permanent spasm, requiring morphine (MST), up to 80 mg a day and

Co-Codamol, as many as were required. Every time I finished a pack, I was phoning and getting more; at one stage, I had more Co-Codamol than a chemist shop. One day about three years ago, I looked in the mirror again and was absolutely shocked at my pallor. I was nearly yellow and looked very unwell. I went to the doctor, and after I explained, she came back with, 'What do you want me to do?' I got up from my chair in real pain and went to sign up with a different practice.

Two days later, I went to see a new doctor and explained the whole deal to him. I was coming off the morphine and Co-Codamol, come hell or high water. I asked my doctor to cut me down by 5 mg a week, knowing I would have a withdrawal every Monday, though not severe. Either I am a better man than I think I am or just plain stubborn, retaining my commando spirit. In sixteen weeks, I was opiate free and using 2 mg of diazepam only when the spasms were too bad. I have bought all sorts of aids for my back; nothing gives anything other than temporary relief. So I just get on with it, sucking in the pain.

I am technically still a member of the Church, thirty-one years later, and have many good friends. However, I found about three in every five loved to natter and gossip, and the same people were given the major 'callings' in the Church. A calling is supposed to come from God, and it is then your 'responsibility' until you are released from it. When you receive a calling, you are called 'president'. My old friend, Tom White, now deceased, said, 'We had more presidents than the Mexican Army!' I felt there were family cliques, and still do. This, to me, ruined the principles I had learnt. On the plus side, I had stopped drugs completely, stopped smoking and drinking.

My son was a typical teenager and hated going to church; nevertheless, he went and also went to Young Men's camps, where I did the same spiel of adventure training and was able to show how close I could get without them realising I was there (about four feet). I had previously, with a friend, ran the initial Young Men's camp. We gave a set of rules which were expected to be adhered too. One young man was like Steven and knew better. Due to the skills of my friend and myself, we stopped him from killing himself in a slip! Imagine then my consternation and extreme anger when the guy I stuck my neck out for became Stake Young Man's President, issued rules which Steven immediately broke, and was instantaneously sent home. I went to speak to him and reminded him of the past. He refused to listen, and as I said, I still have my bad bits and will never be an angel. I will always be honourable though. I let go with the shortest, sweetest right hand I had ever thrown. I had to be pulled off by two other friends, and yes, I still count them as friends. At the end of the day, my attack was seriously wrong, and to the assaulted one's credit, he did not have me charged.

I was always fine until I heard something doctrinal which I did not agree with or had my own opinion on. I would then throw the teddy out of the pram and always find solace in a glass. I have been away from the Church for over three years now, and although I am drinking occasionally, my major joys are weekends which old Army friends have initiated. I am not sure if you could say this about civilian life, but you are accepted, warts and all, by those people. When you meet pals for the first time in over forty years, you actually see joy on their faces at meeting again, and you start talking as if you had never been apart, never mind forty years further down the line.

The Internet has become the greatest tool in my life. Most days, I talk and banter with old friends, getting told off for drinking whilst on medication. I also go collecting for military charities. I had found out that not one penny paid on the streets for 'Help for Heroes' merchandise, sold by collectors, ever goes to the soldiers, and this riled me greatly. I wrote to Perth Racecourse on behalf of 'Veterans in Action', and we were given a whole summer collecting, giving out information on post-traumatic stress disorder. Yes that was a happy summer; our group of five collectors were doing well. The laughs and banter really kept me going—usually at my expense!

I have in no way been the best type of father or husband to my wife of thirty years nor to my children. I am deliberately omitting them, as is their wish. I have always been a worker and a 'trier', however, they know, if I can help, I almost certainly will.

CHAPTER 23

Letting Go!

'Wisdom is nothing more than healed pain. Maybe if I share the path I walk, then a little more of your pain will vanish.

'I want you to heal, whoever you are. I don't care what pain you've brought the world. I just want yours to subside.

'No matter what, your path is yours. Do not follow misery or worry. Devote every moment of your life to improving your dreams.

'Love your world. Cherish the good you do. Let go of hatred. Dream of love.'

—Anonymous

I found the above quote online and knew immediately that it had to be included in this, my final chapter. Victims will feel it more than most, as the mental anguish never leaves you. Quite simply, you are suffering from post-traumatic stress disorder, or PTSD for short. It spills out in many ways; for me, as rage for no apparent reason. Others cry every time the thought comes, yet more 'self-harm' and think they have no worth . . . why? Because some pervert, bully, or abuser seeks to visit their type of harm on you!

http://www.nhs.uk/Conditions/Post-traumatic-stress-disorder/Pages/Symptoms.aspx

I am no psychiatrist, however, be aware. Telling someone you don't know or trust just does not work. It really is akin to a chocolate teapot: People of superior intelligence have usually never been in the world of victims. They merely add a sticking plaster to cover your massive pain edifice. I have found from my own experience, there will come a time when everything spews out in a torrent. However, it will not disappear. Fact! However, you can dilute it simply by getting it out, whether you write it down and burn it, or as I am doing, making it public. We must remember, our brain is a massive filing cabinet. It stores the good and the bad and does not differentiate into which cabinet a specific memory will go. Why do I remember more of the degradation, abuse, bullying, and fear rather than my lifetime abilities and qualities? There are many people who have spent their lives fighting for justice, justice over things like racism, nepotism, and sexism, whether it be Mohammed Ali and many other Afro-American athletes, who, although they went out of their way to win medals and kudos for their country, were in fact ostracised by their nation or others. Soldiers in the trenches were shot for 'cowardice' because they could not go 'over the top' with bayonet fixed. Think please: These men, who were called cowards, had signed up to defend our nation but were in a no-win situation. Go over, they died, stay, and they died. Every single person is born with a 'selfish gene', in my opinion, or we would not fight to live, even when we get to the nadir of our lives. 'Fight or flight', you have your choice.

I asked a few friends, also victims, for their thoughts on the attacks, assaults, and perversions visited upon them. The results were very vivid and eye-opening to me. Yes, there were similarities, the main one being very low self-esteem and the tangled feelings inside. The oddest thing to me is that bullies pick up this sensation and pick on it. I have used excerpts from their experiences:

Friend 1

> As a victim, I felt alone, worthless, betrayed, confused, no confidence or self-esteem, nothing apart from my bastard step-dad's cruelty. I fell foul of the school bullies, who only saw my pain as something to abuse. I only felt partially good about myself when I was bundled off into a care home or put with some family or other but knew it wasn't to last and that I would be sent back to the place where he was. I couldn't make sense of anything and used to lie under my covers in bed in fear, waiting

for him to come in and start. The anxiety and inner fear is still in me, but I have lived with that for so long I don't know what it would be like not to have it. I tried three times as a teenager to end my life and nobody asked why, strange times the 1950s. I was taken to a hospital when I was about seventeen and they put electricity through my brain: ECT, they called it. I called it torture and yet again was suffering another pain; too many things going on inside me, so I got a bit of spark in me and gave the bastard a good hiding and left him and my so-called mother to get on with it. I joined my family, the Army, in March 1962 and spent nine years of happy days. One good thing, though, Bob. I live for my family and will never ever let anybody walk over me again.

Friend 2

Dad came a few times to collect me on end-of-term leave, but I don't think I ever shaped up. Had to leave home really at sixteen, purely because they couldn't afford to keep four children! The ten years I was away put a gulf between me and my parents and between me and my three brothers. Dad doted on two of my brothers: One is a spiv, and the other is a multimillionaire. My youngest brother has had self-esteem problems and stress, and about four years back, the police talked him off Beachey Head. I really picked up on what you said about the self-esteem, and I have fought low self-esteem all my life. Sometimes I think I go out of my way to do things for others because I need their 'vote' or 'friendship', and a lot of the times, I get shafted. However, I have a great wife and two great kids. One is a right go-getter, but my other son, alas, is suffering the genetic 'low esteem' and 'low confidence', probably a trait he has in fact learnt whilst growing up from me.

Friend 3

(This to me was so moving and difficult to read without crying that I have decided to put it all in: Fear and self loathing . . . go hand in hand.)

I can't remember the first time I felt real fear . . . that pit-of-the-stomach, clammy nausea . . . for I have always known it: fear for my mother and brothers . . . the screams behind the closed door, raised angry voices, shouting, screaming, slapping, punching . . . crying, sobbing, and then silence.

Fear of him . . . him coming home . . . how would he be? Drunk . . . obviously . . . but would he demand your presence or would you be allowed to escape out of sight?

Hiding in bed . . . pretending to be asleep . . . silent sobs . . . until sleep came of its own accord.

Fear for myself . . . first time really when I was sixteen . . . standing at the old tin bus shelter . . . a cold November day, blissfully unaware of how that day would change me.

The dirty, sweaty hand that clamped over my mouth from behind was the first I knew what was happening; another hand was clawing at my clothes as both dragged me to the ground, pulling me down. A man's voice mumbling inaudibly in my ear, something about being cold . . . nothing made any sense. Split seconds that seemed to stand still and sheer terror. He was tall . . . much taller than me . . . I remember kicking and biting and trying to scream. However, his hand was glued to my mouth . . . he was big and heavy and smelt of sweat and I seemed powerless. Why? Why me?! What had I done to him? I don't understand! Someone help me . . . someone pass by and see . . . please.

No, don't see . . . I am so ashamed. Please don't let anyone see. Silent tears streamed down my face. I remember looking into his dark, dead eyes and pleading for him to stop . . . that only seemed to make it worse. And almost as suddenly as it started, he was gone . . . I lay on the cold pavement, shaking and crying. Worthless rubbish left on the ground . . . I dragged myself to my feet . . . battered, bruised, ripped, and bleeding. For some silly reason, trying to make myself decent . . . and cover up what had just happened, so ashamed, sobbing . . . ashamed and dirty. For years, I couldn't walk in crowds . . . anyone too close to me, my skin would crawl. I would burst into tears, literally run from places in panic. People must have thought me mad. Almost thirty years on, I still won't stand in a bus shelter if anyone else comes near . . . I stand outside . . . no matter the weather. I can't have anyone put their hand near my mouth without the fear freezing my body . . . fear and the memory of my shame taking over. I got married when I was twenty . . . almost twenty-one. Never had the looks and had only had three boyfriends . . . one serious among them . . . until my husband. Not very worldly wise . . . a bit of an innocent, all things considered. Even through a childhood that knew nothing but violence, school bullies, and a teenage rape . . . still willing to see the best in people, especially this man who seemed to be so loving, attentive, and kind and generous and funny . . . We met and married within ten months, whirlwind, I think they call it. The first time I saw another side to him was 3 July 1988 . . . the day after our wedding. I can't remember what I had said or done to anger him . . . but one minute I was standing at the foot of our new marital bed . . . the next, I was knocked off of my feet with one punch and landed at the headboard . . . banging my head against it . . . I remember the shock . . . What had just happened?!

Then I felt the pain in my arm and realised he had managed to send me flying with one punch. It was the first of many attacks, being thrown down stairs, punched, kicked, throttled, slapped . . . whatever . . . for either some 'reason' or none. Everything, each reason, was inevitably my fault. That's when the fear and the shame came back into my life . . . all too easily, that all too familiar feeling: the knot in the pit of my stomach, like a fist, the cold sweat, the panic, and dread . . . wanting to run . . . but frozen to the spot. The emotional and verbal abuse I think is often worse . . . sounds stupid, but a physical pain is real and something to focus on . . . emotional and verbal abuse eats away at your very being . . . at your self-esteem, self-worth . . . at your soul. Someone recently said to me, 'Think of a time when you last loved yourself' . . . I can honestly say, 'Never.' Self-loathing, shame, and guilt have always been my inward glances; guilt, that I couldn't save my mother from the beatings, even though I was only a child . . . self-loathing, for being afraid and useless . . . shame, that I had somehow caused all these things; that it's my fault. I have no confidence, no value, or worth. The irony is that I detest all that I am . . . not all that has been done to me . . . I hate myself more than my father, my rapist, or my husband. I have 'self-harmed' and thought of suicide many times, with my son being my unwitting saviour. What did these men leave me with? A legacy of self-loathing and self-destruction. Even when they are all long gone . . . I still have to live with the person I hate the most . . . me.

Friend 4

I was born in 1968 in Blackpool. I have one sister and three half-sisters from my mother's first marriage. I, like many, don't recall my first few years. When I slowly became aware, I realised my father was a soldier from pictures around the house.

He, in fact, was a Royal Engineer, and as a result, I was born into the Corps as a 'pads brat', a term used by serving members . . . I recall moving around quite a lot in the early days, starting at new schools and leaving shortly thereafter, making new and losing old friends became the norm. One of the most defining moments of my life happened at Gillingham, the school name escapes me.

I was about six, maybe seven, and it was the norm to walk to school on my own, but on one occasion, I met another boy, and one thing led to another when we went to the corner shop to buy sweets, and the going-to-school bit became a secondary event. I recall walking through a park, swings to my left, slide to my right, when I noticed my father walking towards me. I recall very little of the day; no telling off, nothing. It was that evening when my father took my hand and led me upstairs, pulled my jim-jams bottoms down and took an army green belt to my backside and beat me with it. I screamed and he just continued; there's nothing worse than being held down by someone so much stronger than yourself . . . Then it stopped. He went downstairs and I recall bawling my eyes out for an age . . . recall my mother walked up the stairs and placed a pack of Opel fruits at the top of the stairs. The bruise I carried covered from behind the right knee up to my rib cage, deep true black. Now I remember nothing about my life until my sister and I were left at my first boarding school, which was Harecroft Hall in Cumbria. The sadness I felt was truly low. I rarely saw my sister, as it was a mixed but separated school. At this school, I learnt I had a talent. I was a promising cricketer. I was coached by Gregg Mathews, Australian bowler-batsman. I enjoyed the school in the most part. It was 1979. I learnt later that my father had been posted to Nepal, working on a power station.

This is a country I've had the privilege to live in, as we had three months' holidays . . . truly awesome. My second boarding school was Chilton Cantelo School in Yeovil. I enjoyed my time there. I was doing well then. I recall one day some four years later, with little contact with them, my parents, they had returned, and it was off to Ripon for his next posting. It was there I realised something was wrong: the shouting, the silence between parents, and the level of filth. It started with dust, then we had two dogs, Toby and Pip, little Yorkshire Terriers. Toby was mine. My mum was very quiet all the time. I was to learn later that my father had many affairs. I can't vouch for this. These are stories told by my mum to girlfriends.

The moment of realisation came when my sister and I walked three, maybe four, miles to a fairground by ourselves; this was the norm . . . I spent the pound I was given on a cake for my mum. I walked all the way back with this cake feeling so pleased with myself that this will make her smile. I walked into the house and gave my mum the cake. She didn't even look up, took it, and placed it on a table beside her, and carried on smoking . . . I knew at that moment that both parents didn't care, or that's how I saw it. Our next posting was Gutersloh, Ten Field Squadron RE. There, I sat my exams and, having only been in the school for five months, hadn't been taught half the subjects, passing only one O level. Leaving school and still being at home, the house was becoming so filthy that any friend who came to visit never returned. Loneliness was now becoming my biggest enemy, something that I carry to this day. The conditions were utterly disgusting. On 15 September 1985, I got into my dad's car, a cherry Datsun Estate, which I must say was smoke-filled and filthy. Now, I remember looking back. I noticed how sad my mum was, standing at the front door.

So in the car I went. We travelled all the way through Germany, got on a ferry, landed by some white cliffs, and off we went again and travelled across southern England, when I noticed a road sign: 'Welcome to Wales' across a large bridge (the Severn Bridge), and suddenly, I was at the Army Apprentice

College, Chepstow, the Boys Trade Training Centre for future sappers in the Corps of Royal Engineers. The most prominent point of that journey was we never talked, and I hadn't a clue where I was going . . . I did tests and runs for entrance but truly had no idea where I was. Then he was gone. I would not see my parents until pass-off two years later. We went home and the living conditions were truly shocking. There was dog shit and urine everywhere; it was horrendous. I didn't stay and became a young orphan at Chepstow, staying there when the camp was empty. What surprised me was there were others like me, but at sixteen, you just don't realise their drifts and circumstances. After Chepstow, it was Three Training Regiment Royal Engineers, the combat engineering school, mines bridging defences, and so on; enjoyed it there.

Next, the happiest moments were being posted to Thirty-two Armoured Engineer Regiment, Munstalager, northern Germany. I became an armoured engineer . . . two great years, when in late 1989, a pissed-up full corporal battered me in bed. I saved him from Colchester by relating a bar baseball accident.

He was married with kids, so in my view, he was protected, and I was posted out to Twenty-one Engineer Regiment, Nienburgh. I completed my cadre there and went to the Gulf War 1990-1, but it was also there I realised I had the early signs of a mental illness. I was withdrawn, but mostly angry. What was strange is that I attracted bullies, and then the fighting started. No man was going to hurt me again without a fight . . . but I hated myself. I was kind and never drank before. Now drink could cause the red mist to come down. From Neinburgh, I was posted to Sandhurst, the officer training school in Camberley. There, I was calm and, have to say, enjoyed it. One of the biggest regrets of my life occurred there; I was offered a place as a potential officer.

I had the ability and I'm a very affable person, but damaged as a result of no love as a kid. I said no; if I could turn back time, but hey ho. My next listing was my first tour in Northern Ireland and, for someone now suffering paranoia, not the most ideal place to go. I was promoted there, and I was to lose my best friend at the time Gez Goulding, this I couldn't take, still hurts. I went from Northern Ireland to Ripon with Thirty-eight Engineer Regiment.

I was with the Fifty-one Airmob Squadron. It started badly and it was there I decided I had to leave.

Now, I haven't mentioned my parents. It was 1996. Apart from a couple of visits to my mum and dad, I hadn't seen either since 1994. The shame of them and the conditions they lived in was too much, and I started to realise my anger was directed towards the man who beat me with a belt so bad that in today's situation, he would have got a prison sentence and I would have ended up in care.

He was the reason for my anger; his failings as the first man who should have loved me. He failed.

From Ripon, I started my second tour of Northern Ireland from 1998 to 2000, when I left the Corps.

At that point, my mental health was poor . . . I hated myself, and it must be said, most hated me, except a few, and then, I was the kindest person you could ever meet. Strange that? I left and scratched around for work as a Class 1 LGV driver, when in 2002, I beat off 800 applicants for a Tesco driving job . . . It was at that moment I sought help, and in 2003, I had a breakdown. I was helped by a psychologist, who broke me, made me cry, and started the healing process. I also studied psychology, as I fell in love with the healing process . . . It's now 2012. I have no family other than my wonderful wife and my two sons. I live in a wonderful home. I am not rich, but I'm not poor. I have taken on the world by myself and I am doing very well.

I learnt to smile and for you reading this book, many suffer. It takes great strength to overcome the failings of others, in my case, my mum and dad. I now know it wasn't really their fault. They couldn't cope and were both very ill, and I assume they still are if they are indeed alive. However, I can't help them. I had to let them go. I always wonder how children go missing, but I know how easy it is to happen. There was no one that came looking for me, no uncle, auntie, no one.

So my advice is you must fight, be strong, and keep pushing. Seek help when needed and every moment smile; smile so hard it hurts. Looking back, I love the Corps of Royal Engineers. It taught me the strength to fight and keep on going. Now, my final point, my time has been a blessing in disguise; because of all the failures,

I've learnt how to treat people. My sons are the most spoilt kids on the planet and I adore the woman I married . . .

> With kind regards,
> Gavin Hodge
> Royal Engineers

For me, everything I have read, heard, or transcribed has been like peeling scabs off a wound: It hurts, but underneath, it always looks better.

I am now fifty-seven years old; my marriage is in difficulty. I live in my own room alone, looking at the ceiling and thinking, 'If only.' Each and every single one of us has difficulties, have stories to tell. I still stand tall; I know no fear any more. I pick up on bullying quickly and try to negate it. I became an independent advocate twelve years ago. However, I only did two cases before I had to give up; back came the feelings like a measles epidemic, taking control of my brain. I empathised but cried inside.

My cure began three years ago when I went to my very first 'Remembrance Weekend' since leaving the Army thirty-two years before. It made me realise the special bond that soldiers have, more especially Royal Engineers (sappers). We laughed as one, sang as one, and bonded on the very first meeting. Gentlemen, I salute you; your banter and bonhomie made a huge difference to my life.

It was then I realised my story was going public.

I put it off, like I do with a lot of things. However, on writing the poem 'What Is Hurt?' in five minutes in June this year, my first attempt at anything literary since 1966 Primary, I was given feedback which wowed me and a little bit of self-esteem has come back. Now, as I write this book online, the feedback on chapters astounded me, and my self-esteem came roaring back, screaming at me, 'You are a person of worth.' I had felt the fear of letting go; it was not nice. At times, it was exceedingly uncomfortable. I am me; I will do my best to be me from now onwards. Please, Readers, 'Never judge anyone, anywhere, until you have walked at least ten miles in their shoes.' A mile is far too short a distance to understand the *hurt* of a *victim!* If I can find five friends with this type of hurt in their lives, look out in your friend base. You have some as well. They all require aid, assistance, and love.

I now wish to reiterate those wise words of an anonymous online writer:

> 'Wisdom is nothing more than healed pain. Maybe if I share the path I walk, then a little more of your pain will vanish.
>
> 'I want you to heal, whoever you are. I don't care what pain you've brought the world. I just want yours to subside.
>
> 'No matter what, your path is yours. Do not follow misery or worry. Devote every moment of your life to improving your dreams.
>
> 'Love your world. Cherish the good you do. Let go of hatred.
>
> 'Dream of love.'

INDEX

A

ABA 86, 91
abuse 10, 82, 89, 123, 126
abuse survivors 107
Adams, Eggs 50-1, 53, 56
Addie 42-3, 115
Adkins, Dougal 61
ammunition 73, 93
anger 15, 20, 126, 130
apprentices 49, 51, 64, 66, 70
APTI 77
Arbroath 103
Army boxing team 57, 77, 79-83, 89, 94, 106, 111
assault course 93-4, 101, 110, 123
Aylward, Gladys 37-8

B

Bailey Bridges 66
band 37, 108, 110
Beaumont, Ricky 69
Blomquist, Mick 49
Booth, Charlie 69, 82, 86
borstal 21
boxing 18, 22-5, 30-3, 47-8, 53-5, 67-70, 85-6, 88-9, 106
Brother Bede 35
Brother John 35-7

brothers 83, 99, 124-5
Brown, Charlie 90
Bugner, Joe 86
bullies 31-4, 37, 41, 43, 61-2, 72, 114, 122-3
bullying 12, 31, 33-4, 64, 123, 131
Burns, Alma 10

C

camaraderie 78, 93
camp 33, 52, 54, 57-9, 66-7, 72-3, 75, 78, 95, 98-100, 118, 120, 129
Carlin, Graham 119
Caswell, Billy 25
Catholics 12-13, 63
Chalmers, Mary 42
Charleston 14, 27
Chase, Charlie 54, 56, 60
Chattenden 86-7, 111
Cheetam, John 83
Chepstow 40, 44-7, 49-50, 54, 56-8, 60-1, 66-70, 84, 87, 97, 129
Cherry, Brian Joseph 80, 83, 88, 91-2, 106
China 38
choice 5, 9, 14, 38, 47, 89, 98, 106, 117, 123
church 13, 33, 44, 63, 116, 119-21
Citadel 91-4, 100-1, 107, 111

133

club   23, 25, 33, 106, 110, 117, 119
Co-Codamol   120
cod liver oil   56
college   47, 54, 60, 62, 70, 129
companies   23, 61, 103-4
competition   44, 62-3, 99
Condor   96, 103, 105
Condor Troop   101, 103
Conway, Steve   13
Coombes, David   69
corporal   71, 73, 76, 78-9, 86, 97, 101, 103, 129
Cove   64, 70-1, 74, 77-9, 90, 111
Coyle, Norah   31
Craigmount Road   19-20, 23, 43
craphat   76, 104
Crighton, Alan   23
Crouch, Andy   77-8
Crownhill   96-7, 100, 106
Cummings, Bill   70
Cupar   104, 106
Curran, Bob   5, 9-12, 14-15, 19, 21, 24-6, 28-9, 33, 39, 41-4, 48, 53, 55, 81, 83, 86, 88, 104, 121, 124, 126-8, 130
Curran, Lizzie   42
Curran, Robert   5, 9-12, 14-15, 19, 21, 24, 26, 28-9, 33, 41-4, 124, 127-8, 130
Cypriots   109
Cyprus   99, 108-9, 111

D

Daktari   50-1, 54, 56, 63, 68
Dalton, Tony   97, 101
danger days   28
Davies, Chris   82, 84, 88
decision   21, 44, 68, 86, 88-9, 91
demon   10-11
detonators   74

Dick   11, 14
doctor   22, 33, 111, 113-14, 120
doorman   110
Dorothy   104, 106, 109, 111
drill   54, 61-2, 95, 114
drill and turn-out   62
drugs   115, 119-20
Dryburgh Crescent   12, 18, 20
Dundee   18-19, 36, 43-4, 64, 69, 77, 86, 113-14, 116, 119
Dunshelt   104-5

E

Edwards, Ivan   70
Ellis, Ray   99, 101
endurance   94, 96, 111
equipment   10, 50, 57, 59, 74, 89-90, 94-6, 102-3
excitement   45-6
exercise   72-3, 96, 98-9, 108, 111, 119

F

family   10, 20, 25, 41, 64, 116, 123-4, 130
farmers   27, 58-9
fault   14, 30, 57, 72, 106, 126, 130
fear   11, 14, 30, 42, 46, 79, 123-6, 131
Feeney, George   69, 72, 90
Ferry, George   103
fields   20, 26-8, 36
Fifty-nine Commando   32, 91-2, 102, 109
Fifty-niners   97-8
First Training Regiment   75-6
Fox Lines   77-8
Foy, Chris   82

Frank   40, 42-4, 64, 117
Fusiliers, Irish   53

G

Garlic   119
gays   35, 71, 73, 108
Gilbert, Paul   92, 96
Gimpy   62-3
Gordon, Bombardier   53-5
Gorthy, Ian   97
Green, Dave Boy   86
guardroom   53, 68, 74, 99, 101
guests   60, 62
guilt   12, 126
gym   49, 68, 73, 76-7, 79, 83, 85-6

H

hackles   26, 55, 57, 98
Hall, Frank   52, 63, 67
Hanson, Nanette   36
Harris, Chats   85
Harwood, Eddie   67
Haslett, Paddy   79, 86
head teacher   34
healing process   130
Henney, Jock   61-2
Henry, Frank   72
Higgins, Alex   108
Hines, Tony   68, 70
history   25, 34, 41, 93
hockey   62, 68, 70
Hodge, Gavin   131
Holdsworth, Steve   89, 105
Hopkins, Gaynor   52
hospital   34, 62, 124
Hughes   71-2, 74, 79
Hutchinson, Billy   83
Hutchison, Thomas   28-9

I

Ian   45, 104
Inn of the Sixth Happiness, The   37
inspection   50-1, 94, 107
instrument   37
Ireland   96, 101, 119

J

Japanese patrols   38
Jones   62
Jones, Skip   87
justice   61, 72, 123

K

Kathleen   14
Keirnan, Joe   76-7, 80, 82-3, 85, 90, 106
Kelbie, Frank   21
Kreacher   25

L

Land Rover   57, 99, 101, 103, 110, 112
Langley, Phil   51-3, 58, 64, 67, 69
Leatherhead   89
Leek, Taff   61-2
Li   38
Lilburn, Stewart   35
Lin   38
Lochee   14, 17, 20, 119
Lochee Boys Club   23-4
London   57, 87, 89
lover   106-7
Lympstone   91-2, 94-5, 97, 101
Lynch, Andy   10, 19
Lynch, Ned   23, 86

M

MacDonald, Mac 103-4
Maida Gym 77, 79, 90-1
Major Fields 52-3, 106-7
Mancini, Ray 90
maps 44, 57-8, 93
Martin, Billy 20
Martin, David 20
Martin, Peter 20
Mary (Gran) 18, 42
Matelots 93-6
Mathieson, Matty 54
Matthews, Jimmy 81, 83
Maxwell, Roger 81
McAlpine, Danny 25
McBreartie, Alec 20
McConnachie, Adam McKay 42
McDonald, Stelios 110
McFarlane, Dave 68
McFee, Nanny 12
McGiveron, Terry 106
McKenzie, Clinton 69
McKillen, Matt 35
McMaster, Don 92
McMillan, Tom 20
Mehrlich, Paul 77
Mid Craigie 27
migrants 22, 27
Mone, Robert Francis 35-6
Monroe, Jim 22-3
Moorhouse, John 76, 79
morphine 119-20
mother 5, 9-12, 14-15, 19, 21-2, 27, 33, 41, 43-4, 86, 105, 124-8, 130
Mr Barr 28-9
Muir, Jock 86
Munro, Bob 103
Murray, Punchy 101, 107, 111

N

NAAFI 48, 53, 64, 79, 86-7
Navy 21, 84-5, 93
needlework class 36
neighbours 11, 22, 26-7, 29, 37, 98, 114
nepotism 123
Northern Ireland 92, 129-30
nuns 13, 32

O

O'Brien, Keith Patrick 16
O'Brien, Moss 89
officer commanding (OC) 52-3, 108
Ogierman, Alex 11
opponent 23-4, 69, 90-1
O'Shaugnessy, Mick 53
Oswestry 54, 56, 68
Ouzo 110

P

Packer, Nigel 61
paedophiles 26, 29-30, 70-1
pain 5, 29-30, 53, 111, 120, 122-4, 126, 132
Pederson, Al 97-8, 103
perverts 35, 122
Phillips, Norman 77, 81
Phillips, Steve 84
Phinn, Hazel 37
Pickles, Steve 91, 111
Pip 128
platform 45-7, 86, 112
platoon 47-9, 54, 61-2, 69, 79
Plymouth 91, 102, 106-7, 110-11, 113
Pogson, Ian 97, 104

police 5, 14, 19-21, 28, 36, 43, 57, 102, 115, 119, 124
Pope 35-6, 39
post-traumatic stress disorder 121-2
posting 75, 79, 128
president 120
pride 50, 55, 62, 94-5, 99, 113
prison revolt 38
private function 110
pub 9, 64, 93, 99-100
punches 22, 29, 43, 79, 90, 126

R

Rab 10, 14, 42
racism 123
Rainey, Paddy 96
referee 84-5, 90
Restriction of Privileges (ROPs) 53
Rizzio 39
Robinson 38
rounds 55, 77, 83, 85, 89-90, 95
Royal Engineers 45, 79, 86-8, 127, 131
Royal Green Jackets 81, 83
Royal Marines (Booties) 93-5, 97
rules 29, 58, 72, 103, 120
Rutherford, Les 97, 99

S

safety 9, 36, 38, 40, 66
sailor 94-5
Sands, Danny 27, 30
Sands, Fiona 27
sappers 64, 66, 83, 93, 101-2, 106, 108, 129, 131
scales 23, 26, 51, 69
school 12-13, 31-7, 39-40, 42, 85, 113, 127-8

school bullies 57, 123, 126
score 83, 99
Scots 27
Scott, Jim 23
Seaton Barracks 92, 112
self-control 107
self-esteem 30-1, 44, 91, 107, 123-4, 126, 131
self-loading rifle (SLR) 93, 96
self-loathing 126-7
sex 29, 107
sexism 123
shame 20, 126, 130
Sister Mary Angela 12-13, 33
Slaven, Tommy 49, 53
Smee, Geoff 91
Smith, Allan 23-4
Smith, Andy 86
Smith, Billy 10
Snodland 87
soldiers 58, 78, 91, 121, 123, 127, 131
Spain 41
sparring 23, 33, 119
Spike 27
Spiral Staircase, The 11
sports 18, 23, 57, 61, 70, 87, 108
squadron 72, 74-5, 85, 87, 92, 101-2, 110, 112
square 62, 70, 93, 96
St Clement's Primary School 12-13, 35
St John's 35-6, 39
staff 53, 73, 84, 87, 93, 96-8
Stewart, Ed Stewpot 88
stories 15, 24, 29, 35, 37-8, 43, 56, 62, 89, 117, 128, 131
stupidity 105
Swampy 20-1

T

Tam 12, 64-5
tank tracks 76-7, 82
teachers 33-7, 60
team 20-1, 25, 31, 49, 54, 62, 80-3, 90-1, 94-9, 101, 103, 106
terms 51, 54-6, 58, 60-1, 63, 67-70, 79, 105, 127
tests 49, 73, 85, 93, 95-6, 129
Tina 34
Toby 128
Tommy 14
trade training 54, 56, 67
travel warrant 58
Traynor, Tom 25
trepidation 45-6
trials 93
troop 73-4, 96-100, 103, 108, 110

V

veterans 99-100
victims 5, 15, 25, 29-30, 45, 56, 67, 105, 122-3, 131
Victoria Cinema 37
volunteers 41, 94, 100

W

Wakeman, Rick 88
Wales 67, 82, 86, 88, 90
Wall, John 88
Wallace, Wally 68
wars 33, 41-2
weapons 93, 95-6, 98, 101, 116
weigh-in 69, 82
Welsh 62, 88, 90
White, Tom 120
Will, Alex 25
Williams, Dave 47-50, 52, 58, 101
Wilson, Peter 23
Winn, Tony 68
winners 37, 82-4, 99, 103
Witchy Poo 21
World War II 41, 66

Y

Yates, Sapper 57
yeast extract 56, 68
York 45, 47
youths 118-19

Lightning Source UK Ltd.
Milton Keynes UK
UKOW050020260113

205388UK00002B/67/P